THE LIBRARY OF AFRICAN-AMERICAN BIOGRAPHY

John David Smith, editor

Louis Armstrong

Louis Armstrong

THE SOUNDTRACK OF
THE AMERICAN EXPERIENCE

David Stricklin

*The Library of
African-American Biography*

IVAN R. DEE · CHICAGO

LOUIS ARMSTRONG. Copyright © 2010 by David Stricklin. All rights reserved, including the right to reproduce this book or portions thereof in any form. For information, address: Ivan R. Dee, Publisher, 1332 North Halsted Street, Chicago 60642, a member of the Rowman & Littlefield Publishing Group.

www.ivanrdee.com

Photographs courtesy of the New Orleans Jazz Club Collection at the Louisiana State Museum.

Library of Congress Cataloging-in-Publication Data:
Stricklin, David, 1952–
  Louis Armstrong : the soundtrack of the American experience / David Stricklin.
    p. cm. — (Library of African-American biography)
  Includes index.
  ISBN 978-1-56663-836-4 (cloth : alk. paper)
  1. Armstrong, Louis, 1901–1971. 2. Jazz musicians—United States—Biography. 3. African American jazz musicians—Biography. I. Title.
  ML419.A75S86 2010
  781.65092—dc22
  [B]   2009042997

To my sisters, Nancy Stricklin Willis and Judy Stricklin

Contents

Preface

IT WILL BE EASIER to understand this book if the reader can listen to the music described in these pages. Please see the section titled Recordings at the end of the book and explore the great body of work Louis Armstrong created and helped create, often with some of the most talented and innovative artists in the United States.

I make extensive use in these pages of Armstrong's own writings. He was an enthusiastic letter writer and memoirist with a distinctive, often eloquent writing style. From piece to piece in his writing, however, there is considerable variation in punctuation, spelling, and other usage practices. I quote him verbatim; the reader should not be distracted by the inconsistencies. See the Note on Sources at the end of the book for comments on various theories about Armstrong's writing.

Armstrong called himself "Louis" (spoken like "Lewis"), not "Louie." He claimed that white people and those who did not know him well called him "Louie," though in fairness it should be pointed out that his wives and quite a few of his friends often called him that. I am convinced that he called himself Louis, not Louie, except when singing songs that used the word or otherwise performing from a script written by someone else. As a matter of respect for the great artist, I suggest readers pronounce his name the way he did.

I wish to thank my great former professor and doctoral adviser, Bill C. Malone, for inspiration and guidance over many years of talking about music and books about music and musicians. His excellent work on Southern music has inspired countless students for decades and been a source of illumination to many general readers. One of the greatest of Bill's achievements is that his writings pass muster in the scholarly community yet remain accessible to the average reader.

Special thanks to Bruce Raeburn for a sensitive reading of the manuscript and for many helpful suggestions.

I would also like to thank the many people with whom I have had the pleasure of playing music over the years, especially Pat Odom, William Daniel, Landa Sloan, Michael Jay, Gary Atchley, Ronnie Norman, Woody Kemp, Larry Barker, Allen Atkinson, Jay Walters, Warren Nelson, Dennis Keys, David Bates, Kathy Johnson, Vernon and Norman Solomon, Ernie Mills, Edward Hopkins, Bob Gregg, Steve Booth, Steve Barnes, Ken Harrell, Dick Chorley, Daryl Powell, Wes Westmoreland and family, Bill and Bobbie Malone, Russell and Nadiene Van Dyke, Mary Howell, Bob and June Lambert, Pat Flory, Charles Chamberlain, Darla R. and Eddie Durham, Barbara Cook, Michael Frisch, Doug Lambert, John Baird, Kenton Adler, Albert Junior Fulks, Danny Dozier, Micky Rigby, Jim Chlebak, Bill Worthen, Tom Fennell, Herb Rule, Mary McGowan, David Austin, and Chris Stewart.

I also want to pay tribute to my musical family: my late grandfather Meeks Stricklin, great uncles John and Will Benton, and aunt Violet Stricklin, who showed me the first guitar and piano chords I ever learned; my late parents, Betty Stricklin, who owned the first Louis Armstrong recording I ever heard, and Al Stricklin, who played music in a famous western swing band but always considered himself a jazz musician; my daughters, Annie Bowyer Stricklin and Sarah

Browder Stricklin, who are truly gifted musicians; my wife, Sally Browder, who has not only taught me a great deal about music but also tolerated my often maddeningly eclectic musical tastes for more than three decades; my mother-in-law, Wilma Browder; my sisters-in-law, Gwen Richardson, Jeanine Johnson, and Peggy Collins, along with Gwen's husband, Jesse Richardson, and various musical Browder grandchildren and cousins; my cousin Bill Laatsch; my niece Leigh Anne Willis Bedrich, nephews Jerry and Robert Willis, and musical great nephews and nieces; my brother-in-law Jerry R. Willis; and my sisters, Nancy Stricklin Willis and Judy Stricklin. In one way or another, through their playing and singing, they all have taught me much about music and what it means to people. To my sisters, I dedicate this book.

Louis Armstrong

Introduction

AFRICAN AMERICANS have distinguished themselves in a wide variety of endeavors, from science and technology to business and industry, to philanthropy and ethics, to arts and letters. In the twentieth century their influence on the performing arts in the United States was so profound that, it has been said, they helped make popular music the soundtrack of the American experience and American music the preeminent force in the world's popular culture. Vast numbers of gifted African-American musicians deserve credit for this remarkable turn of events, but a few stand out as true giants: Scott Joplin, Bessie Smith, W. C. Handy, Duke Ellington, Ella Fitzgerald, Sister Rosetta Tharpe, Louis Jordan, Charlie Parker, Miles Davis, Ray Charles, Sam Cooke, Aretha Franklin. This book explores the life of one such giant, Louis Armstrong.

This is not to say that Armstrong was the best or most important musician of them all, though one of his biographers, James Lincoln Collier, calls him "the preeminent musical genius of his era." My purpose is to set Armstrong apart as a special representative of these remarkable musicians. The life story of this great instrumentalist, bandleader, and entertainer illustrates much of the black experience in the United States and illuminates the ways popular culture often intersects with political and economic forces in American history.

Armstrong emerged from a most precarious background and triumphed over almost impossible odds. At dozens of moments early in his life, he simply could have disappeared, a promising talent crushed by disadvantage, a remarkable personality consigned to anonymity, a legend never known, a story never told. The fact that he persisted, that he made a life for himself, tells something important about the African-American experience. The fact that he became an international icon tells something important about a remarkable individual. Many observers have called Armstrong a genius; this book will explore his very great talent.

But I will also pay special attention to his identity as an African American and to the ways he triumphed over the mistreatment and disrespect so often given to people very much like him. Many of these people did not have his considerable gifts, but some of them may indeed have had them but simply lost or never enjoyed the opportunities to overcome adversity as Armstrong did, never had the chance to show the nation and the world what remarkable people they were. I often wonder how many Ella Fitzgeralds, how many Sam Cookes, how many Louis Armstrongs lived out their time in virtual anonymity because they never got the breaks, never had anyone take them aside and try to better them, never had the chance to share their gifts with the world. This is the story of someone who did get some breaks, who had someone take him aside—several people, in fact—and who got the chance to show what he could do. What he showed and what he shared were his own creations, the expression of his unique and lively sense of freedom. He might have been able to demonstrate that sense in many lines of work, but his story is different and has special power and importance because he expressed it through music.

CHAPTER ONE

Humble Origins

∫⅌⏞ Gary Giddins, one of his biographers, says Louis Armstrong was "raised in a house of cards in the middle of a gale." He was born on August 4, 1901—not July 4, 1900, as he claimed throughout his life—in a modest house on an unremarkable street called Jane's Alley, between Perdido and Poydras streets in the Third Ward, west of downtown New Orleans. His parents were both teenagers. His mother was probably about fifteen years old when Armstrong was born. Her name was Mary Ann ("Mayann") Albert, and she came from a small town west of New Orleans in a sugar-cane-growing region. Armstrong was abandoned by his father, William Armstrong, not long after his birth. Neither Louis nor his younger sister Beatrice ("Mama Lucy") ever knew much about their father. They spent time with him only sporadically and then mainly after he had started another family with another woman.

When Louis was a toddler, his mother moved to a house closer to downtown New Orleans, a squalid neighborhood he wrote about later in life, where women frequently earned money through prostitution in the city's mostly legal Storyville "red light" district. The neighborhood was so tough it was called "the battlefield." Everyone lived in ramshackle houses and used communal outhouses located in one of the yards—as he said, "one side for the men and one side for the women." For the first five years of his life, Louis's mother left him in the care of his grandmother. He always suspected that his mother earned money as a prostitute to support him and his sister when they were young, though she was careful not to let herself be seen by family or friends in the company of disreputable people. Armstrong always gave her credit for doing her best to bring up her children in trying circumstances and maintaining the respect of the people who knew her from the neighborhood and from occasional involvements in church. He had respect for neighborhood women, no doubt including prostitutes, who looked out for him and helped bring him up.

One thing there was plenty of: music. Louis's mother's house was just down the street from Union Sons Hall, famous to music lovers black and white as Funky Butt Hall. Within a few minutes were some of the other key New Orleans honky-tonks such as Odd Fellows Hall, Matranga's, and others well known and faithfully frequented by the rough sorts of people who loved the music but also loved the life the music advertised. People on the margins of society hung around the honky-tonks looking for action—a fast buck, a cheap drink, the company of a prostitute, the opportunity to prove something by fighting somebody, the chance to blend into a crowd and lose the sense, for at least a while, that normal life held little promise. People somewhat better off, and sometimes much better off, hung around these places because it was exciting, exotic, dangerous, and scandalous, though it was difficult to scandalize most folks in a place as loose as New Orleans.

Mayann did not start out in this world. She had come from Boutte, a small town in a Creole area up the Mississippi River from New Orleans. Creole culture in Louisiana provided a comfortable life for many, including quite a number of mixed-race Creoles, many of whom spoke French as well as English and gained good educations and had fairly substantial amounts of money. In fact, Creoles of color had often held a relatively high social standing and a measure of political power in New Orleans. Mayann's life was not like that. Her only options for making a living were working the sugarcane fields near Boutte, long one of the hardest and most dangerous jobs in Southern agriculture, or moving to the city to seek domestic work. She arrived in New Orleans with next to nothing. After probably several years of working as a prostitute, she managed to get out of that line of work and began cleaning houses and taking in laundry.

Despite his mother's efforts to keep him on the right track, Louis had a precarious early life. He avoided falling into most of the traps that engulfed many other boys and never spent large amounts of time in rough company. He went to church occasionally and for several years attended the Fisk School for Boys. The Fisk School had a pretty decent academic program, and Louis attended long enough to learn to read and write. But he was a lackluster student who frequently missed school. His sporadic attendance carried him essentially through about the fifth grade, which had to do in part with the fact that he had to help his mother and sister eke out a living. He did odd jobs around the neighborhood and learned to shoot craps. He did this often and skillfully enough to claim later in life that he had helped support his family with dice. He hung around the honky-tonks, especially Funky Butt Hall, listened to the music from outside, watched the dancing when he could peek in, and observed a great deal of the raw night life of an uninhibited slice of the population. He also got into trouble for fighting and for minor thievery, and showed many of the tendencies for mischief that were known to attract the attention of the police.

He also sang on the streets for pocket change. Many kids in New Orleans did so. The sidewalk performers of New

Orleans created a musical subculture almost as vivid as the one being offered in the honky-tonks and houses of prostitution where jazz was being born at the same time. These young musicians wandered the streets, playing anywhere they could and creating a kind of music no one had heard before. It was wild, and it seemed as if the musicians were making up a great deal of it as they went along. A particularly influential set of these street musicians was called the Spasm Band, a seven-member group that inspired numerous imitators. As Armstrong biographer Laurence Bergreen writes, "They frequently punctuated their music with howls and growls and wild calls to one another, or to their audiences gathering on the sidewalk outside the brothels and gambling joints."

Their carrying on must have attracted as much attention as the music they played. But regardless of the quality of their sounds, they soon had a following. In fact they created an entire category of street performance, for "spasm bands" sprang up all around the entertainment districts of New Orleans. It is quite likely that Armstrong's performance style as an adult, which featured a great deal of carrying on—joking around, making funny faces, laughing enthusiastically—came about in part as a result of seeing the impact of the spasm bands on street audiences. He had to have been impressed by their ability to gather a crowd and hold its attention with everything else going on around them. It was one thing to hold a crowd that had come to see a band play in a regular performance venue, quite another to hold it when all the people had to do if they weren't impressed was to keep walking.

Two things kept Louis from falling into a marginal life with so many of his peers: strong role models and music. The role models came from his family, especially his mother and her cousin Isaac ("Uncle Ike") Myles. At first glance his mother may seem an unlikely candidate for a role model, but it was in part a testimony to Louis's open-minded, non-judgmental outlook that he looked up to her anyway. He ignored anything that other people might have considered shady about her ways of earning money for the family early in his life. His Uncle Ike inspired him by relating the horrors of slavery that Ike's ancestors had endured, especially pointing out the ways slavery turned black people against one another as they tried to gain small advantages in the wretched, demeaning system that robbed them of their labor and their self-respect. Myles also drilled into Louis his strong view that a background of slavery was not an excuse for people to feel sorry for themselves.

With its schizophrenic form of black-white relations, New Orleans offered African Americans more than the usual frustrations experienced by blacks who worked the farms of the South. Out in the country, black families often had white neighbors who were only slightly better off—if at all—than they were, yet were nonetheless viewed as socially superior. As bad as that was, at least in rural areas the relative similarity in economic condition between the races among the farming population helped lessen the sting that African Americans felt from such social inequity. In New Orleans, African Americans of modest or low income had to deal with the fact that many black New Orleanians were quite affluent, something that often led to intraracial prejudice even more galling than the slights and snobbery of whites. Not so long before, a fairly sizable number of African Americans in New Orleans had held slaves, intermarried with whites (many of whom were well-to-do), and enjoyed a social status sometimes rivaling the city's white upper crust for prominence and notoriety. Many poorer blacks had allowed this legacy of bondage, second-class citizenship, maltreatment, and hatred to turn them against whites. But Louis managed to emerge from his childhood and navigate a long career that demanded getting along with white people. He did this without succumbing to the bitterness that caused many young African Americans to refuse to participate in anything connected with the white-run business establishment. One reason he was able to avoid this problem was the influence of a kindly Jewish family.

Aware at a very early age of the poverty that afflicted his family, Louis felt the press of having to earn money. He was aided in this and in a great deal of the formation of his character by good examples of decency and basic humanity he witnessed in a neighboring Jewish family. He always spelled their name as "Karnofsky," though there is some disagreement among Armstrong experts about the correct spelling of the family name. Russian immigrants who arrived in the United States with precious little, the Karnofskys had settled in the poor neighborhood where Armstrong's family lived and befriended the young boy and his family when Armstrong was seven years old. He played with their children and worked with them in the family's business of buying and selling scrap metal and other items. He took many meals in their home and enjoyed the stories and music that pervaded their family life. Armstrong always spoke highly of the Karnofskys. In a very real sense they provided him with his first sustained opportunities for earning a living, which steered him away from the petty crime he had dabbled in.

They also gave him his first exposure to the possibility that he could become a musician. He always said he gained a love of singing in their home, but they also paid him the first money he ever earned as a musician and advanced him the five dollars he needed to purchase his first cornet. He recalled the music in their home in a piece he wrote in 1969, published in a book edited by Thomas Brothers called *Louis Armstrong, in His Own Words*: "The Jewish people have such wonderful souls. I always enjoyed everything they sang and still do. . . . When Mrs. Karnofsky would start singing these words to 'Russian Lullaby' we all would get our places and sing it. So soft and sweet. Then bid each other good night. They were always warm and kind to me, which was very noticeable to me—just a kid who could use a little word of kindness . . ." With the family's encouragement, he began trying to teach himself to play the cornet the Karnofskys helped him buy.

At about the age of eleven, feeling the tug of music, Louis quit school and began hanging around the dance halls and bars where musicians played. He prowled around various honky-tonks in and near his neighborhood, looking for work and for someone who would teach him enough to get a foothold in the music business. He followed the great musicians Joe Oliver and Sidney Bechet around and asked them and others for tips on musical technique. Although Bechet was just four years older than Louis, he looked up to him and longed for his approval. Armstrong later gave Oliver credit for being particularly kind to him. In *Louis Armstrong, in His Own Words*, he says, "He was a wonderful man indeed. I can remember way back in New Orleans, Louisiana, when I was just a boy I used to go to the grocery for Mrs. Stella Oliver (his wife) and when I'd return with Mrs. Oliver's grocery King Oliver [the nickname he later acquired] would give to me a music lesson free as his thanks. I would much rather the lesson than to get the cash monies."

He was proud to have won a certain amount of notice from Oliver, one of a handful of exceedingly important musicians in New Orleans, and remembered getting considerable advice on how to play music and how to make it in a band. He never forgot Oliver's kindness, saying in 1954 in his book *Satchmo: My Life in New Orleans*, "I was just a punk kid when I first saw him, but his first words to me were nicer than everything that I've heard from any of the bigwigs of music." Oliver and Bechet, who went on to become world-famous musicians, both later acknowledged that they recognized Armstrong's talent when he was quite young; but he was such a little kid that neither they nor other aspiring musicians gave him much time or attention. Having left school and the employ of the Karnofskys, and spending more time out of sight of his mother, Louis began to get into trouble again.

A life-changing event came upon him in an odd way on New Year's Day 1913. He was arrested for disturbing the peace, having fired a borrowed pistol into the air in celebration of the New Year. The police, who probably knew him and knew he was not really a very bad boy, kept him in jail overnight and then turned him over to the Colored Waif's Home for Boys. He was frequently assigned to the home after minor offenses well into his teen years. In some ways, instead of signaling the beginning of a life of crime and imprisonment, being in the home was the best thing that could have happened to him. The home provided musical opportunities, a relative stability and kindness insisted on by some of the home's staff and leadership, and discipline. It was run by a former army officer named Joseph Jones, who earned a reputation throughout the city for his benevolent treatment of the boys in his care and his ability to keep the home going with the barest of budgets, which he often supplemented from his own meager salary. He insisted the boys in the home learn something about personal integrity, adopt a daily routine so they could have what for many of them was their first experience of order, and take earnest steps to learn a trade.

Armstrong found the place a welcome change after some of the tricky situations he had witnessed already in his young life. In *Satchmo* he says, "The Waif's Home was surely a very

Louis Armstrong, circled, at age ten with the Waif's Home Band, 1913. The discipline and rudiments of music he learned at the home served him for the rest of his life.

clean place, and we did all the work ourselves. That's where I learned how to scrub floors, wash and iron, cook, make up beds, do a little of everything around the house. The first thing we did to a newcomer was to make him take a good shower, and his head and body were carefully examined to see that he did not bring any vermin into the House. . . . One day a couple of small kids had been picked up in the streets of New Orleans covered with body lice and head lice. Out in the back yard there was an immense kettle that was used to boil up our dirty clothes. Those two kids were in such a filthy condition that we had to shave their heads and throw their clothes into the fire underneath the kettle. . . . Every day we had to line up for inspection.

"Anyone whose clothes were not in proper condition was pulled out of line and made to fix them himself. Once a week we were given a physic [laxative], when we lined up in the morning, and very few of the boys were sick. The place was more like a health center or a boarding school than a boys' jail."

In addition to domestic skills, the home offered instruction in various kinds of manual labor but also in music. And it had a band, mostly consisting of brass instruments. The band's director, Peter Davis, gave Louis his first serious music lessons and spent much of his personal time tutoring the young musician, whose enormous potential Davis recognized and went to great lengths to develop. Louis had done a fair amount of singing on the streets to pick up money. With some of his friends he had a quartet that was recognized for its singing ability and its inventive use of homemade rhythm instruments and horns. So he already had fairly extensive experience singing and playing music around town, at least as a high-level amateur, when he went into the Colored Waif's Home for Boys for the first time.

At the home, though, Louis received his first consistent training in the rudiments of musical technique. Peter Davis eventually settled on the cornet as Louis's principal instrument, which pleased the boy greatly. But at first Louis believed Davis was not fond of him, thinking Davis had heard of his reputation for getting into trouble. In fact, Armstrong writes in *Satchmo*, "Mr. Davis thought that since I had been raised in such bad company I must also be worthless. From the start he gave me a very hard way to go, and I kept my distance. One day I broke an unimportant rule, and he gave me fifteen hard lashes on the hand. After that I was really scared of him for a long time." But Davis had also heard stories of Armstrong's musical ability, which were confirmed when Louis did well in a singing group at the home.

It was only a matter of time until Louis got his chance. He truly longed to be in the band and moped around for six months while Davis made him wait. When Davis finally took him into the band, he started him on the tambourine, which disappointed Louis terribly. He had wanted to get his hands on the brass and begin the process of learning to play like his heroes. But Davis wanted him to start with a rhythm instrument to give him a sense of the most basic elements of music. Later, when he began to play the cornet, he never learned to form a proper embouchure, the positioning of the lips and the use of facial muscles to control the pitch, texture, and volume of the notes played on a wind instrument. This failure led later in life to the famous ruination of his upper lip. But more good things than bad happened, and he quickly demonstrated his great talent at the Waif's Home, especially his ability to pick up melodies and play harmony by ear.

The fact that the Waif's Home band played a wide variety of music helped form Armstrong's personality as a professional musician. The band made public performances playing patriotic songs and marches along with classical pieces, hymns, and sentimental songs from the Victorian popular song list. Armstrong recalls in *Satchmo*, "Mr. Davis made the boys play a little of every kind of music." One thing they did not play, however, was jazz, for two reasons. First, the raucous low-class music would have been considered inappropriate for the earnest young musicians of the Waif's Home. Second, jazz scarcely existed. The music Joe Oliver and Sidney Bechet played was just on its way to becoming jazz. The legendary cornet player Charles "Buddy" Bolden was playing what might be called proto-jazz in places where Armstrong could have heard him. Indeed, Armstrong claimed to have heard Bolden, who was credited early in Armstrong's career with having ignited the revolutionary fires that gave rise to jazz.

Whether Louis heard Bolden or not, he certainly knew musicians who had heard him and even played with him. It is impossible to know whether Bolden's playing had any direct influence on Louis, but it would seem extremely likely that Bolden influenced players who would have influenced Armstrong. In fact, Armstrong's claims to have heard the shadowy Bolden always seemed at least somewhat plausible because of the considerable detail he offered about Bolden's strengths and weaknesses as a horn player: "Old Buddy Bolden blew so hard that I used to wonder if I would ever have enough lung power to fill one of those cornets. All in all Buddy Bolden was a great musician, but I think he blew too hard. I will even go so far as to say he did not blow correctly. In any case he finally went crazy." Bolden did indeed spend his final years, which should have been his heyday, in an insane asylum. But he was still called by many the "first man of jazz" and hailed by his fellow New Orleans musicians as a powerful performer in the transition period between the music of the nineteenth century and that of the twentieth. He was a much-sought-after performer of ragtime, which was all the rage at the time, and he helped show how ragtime could be elaborated and turned into something even more exciting.

But how much the music of New Orleans at this time resembled what people recognized a few years later as jazz is impossible to say. The recording technology of the day was only beginning to be used in New Orleans, and therefore no widely available recordings of the music were made until 1917. About the only thing we know is that the music of New Orleans in the first two decades of the twentieth century was different from the forms—mainly blues and ragtime—that had led up to it. James Lincoln Collier says this fact is important to any attempt to understand Louis Armstrong, who not only did not play jazz in his formative years but never considered himself "just" a jazz musician. In fact, Collier says, given Armstrong's international fame as a great jazz performer, "It is one of the great paradoxes of jazz that

Louis Armstrong did not really consider himself primarily a jazz player."

A crucial factor in Louis's development as a musician was the diversity of music he learned to play from the very beginning. This became one of his greatest strengths as a musician, one of the sources of his wide popularity later in life, and one of the central reasons he drove critics crazy after first supplying them for years with important breakthroughs in jazz. His experience in the Waif's Home band points up another crucial factor in Armstrong's early development: this was the first real notice he ever won as a musician. For the rest of his life, playing music was the most important thing he did, the source of his identity as a person, and the way he shared his unique manner of joy with countless people. He owed a great deal to the Waif's Home.

Gary Giddins describes testimony that accounts for some of Armstrong's frequent assignments to the home, particularly his habit of stealing newspapers from white boys who sold them on the city's streetcars. There is no direct evidence that Armstrong stole the newspapers as an act of protest, but it certainly must have galled him to see boys his own age making a decent living doing something he was prevented from doing because he was black. Giddins says selling newspapers "was a 'white-only' job, . . . and whenever Louis was seen leaving a streetcar with papers under his arm, he was arrested and returned to the Waif's Home." No direct testimony confirms that Armstrong stole the papers so he would be sent back to the home. But he was relatively happy there, grateful for the semblance of normality it gave his otherwise chaotic existence, and probably relieved to get a break from having to help provide an income for his struggling family.

He was also, of course, especially grateful for the musical opportunities the Waif's Home provided him. In *Satchmo* he tells how proud he was when for the first time the band paraded through his old neighborhood, "All the whores, pimps, gamblers, thieves, and beggars were waiting for the band because they knew that Dipper [short for "Dippermouth," one of his many nicknames] would be in it. They never dreamed that I would be playing the cornet, blowing it as good as I did." He spoke fondly of the home for the rest of his life and especially praised it for helping him learn something about discipline, which served him well as his career developed. He stayed in touch with the staff of the home and made charitable contributions to it after he became a successful musician.

After his periods in residence at the home, Louis moved in with his father and his new family for a while. He was not happy to leave the Waif's Home and for the most part not happy to live with his father. So he moved back in with his mother. As a teenager, however, he had a fairly high degree of freedom and roamed the city looking for interesting music, which was everywhere, at least in the New Orleans of the day. The city's orientation toward amusement and good times meant there were constant sources of music available, often free. Merely walking down the street in a residential neighborhood could offer a music lover a dizzying array of music, as people played instruments and sang on their front stoops and porches. The city's ever-present marching brass bands made their way to and from events where they performed or sometimes just marched so people could hear them play. No one was ever more than a few minutes' walk from one of the dozens of bars or dance halls or bordellos where musicians were constantly engaged, keeping patrons happy by providing the latest tunes and "jazzing up" or "ragging" the old ones.

Humble beginnings gave Louis many things: an awareness of the need to work hard, a clear vision of the life he might have ahead of him if he did not make something of himself, and the role music might play in his future. It was a priceless opportunity to see at such an early age the possibilities that lay before him and what he had to do in order to reach those possibilities. He had seen his future, and he knew without any doubt that it lay in the pursuit of a career in music. He was signing up for a revolution, though no one, including Louis, knew it at the time.

CHAPTER TWO

A Rising Talent

It is impossible to know exactly what the music that appealed to Armstrong sounded like, but many authorities contend that something akin to jazz was developing in New Orleans in the early 1900s. Many musicians who became jazz pioneers in these years were expanding on the ragtime tunes that had created a frenzy of popularity in the late 1890s and early years of the twentieth century. This trend can be appreciated by listening to piano-roll recordings of ragtime and comparing them to recordings of jazz from the 1920s. The process was gradual—evolutionary at first rather than revolutionary—and many other influences and strands of music gave rise to jazz in New Orleans, especially blues songs, gospel tunes, and the marches of military bands.

It was a somewhat mysterious process, made even more complicated by the remarkable ethnic diversity of New Orleans. Much more than simply a black-and-white town, New Orleans kept one foot in the Latin American world. Its history included a time as a Spanish colony, and its placement as the principal port for goods moving from the Gulf of Mexico up the Mississippi River and into the heartland of the United States gave it traffic to and from the entire Caribbean rim. Its docks teemed with sailors from around the world, some of whom stayed in New Orleans to make their lives. Its Creole past and connections to pirates, voodoo, and every kind of sensual debauchery attracted colorful characters who added much to the city's atmosphere of creativity and experimentation. Its strong identity with Roman Catholicism gave it a religious overlay blending the rhythms of the church year with the constant possibility of forgiveness for sins, providing solace for many. The city's role as the site of a major battle in the War of 1812 (though one that occurred after the war had officially ended) and its occupation by Union troops during the Civil War gave it a military heritage that included marching and march music, especially the use of drums. The various religious folk, Catholics and others, put the profound stamp of their music on the city. Latin Americans added the sounds and rhythms of their traditions. Masking as "Mardi Gras Indian" tribes, African Americans celebrated the legends of Native Americans who helped pre–Civil War blacks in New Orleans get in touch with their African past through drumming. The swirl of musical influences that gave rise to jazz in New Orleans is in fact quite dizzying. The social and cultural effects of that music were equally so.

Something else was going on, though, in the United States as a whole. In the last third of the nineteenth century, American income levels rose as the great industrial corporations solidified their dominance of the nation's economy. One of the consequences was the rise of an urban middle class. At the dawn of the nineteenth century, the overwhelming majority of Americans lived in rural areas and made their living keeping farms. By the end of the century, vast numbers of people had moved to cities to work in factories. Their farm work was performed with astonishing efficiency by fewer people, working with machines made in the urban factories. Their numbers were increased by the influx of immigrants, mostly from Europe, hoping to escape poverty, degradation, and despair. For the people who flocked to work in factories, their dangerous, dirty, often mind-numbingly boring work was nonetheless an improvement over what they had been doing. Many of them made enough money to take the first steps toward the better lives they wanted, and they did something else too. They helped advance the middle class by creating the need for managers to oversee this new industrial production, provide the services, and sell the consumer goods that industrial workers needed and wanted. The new middle class sought ways to distinguish themselves from the rough workers and farmers whose labor helped create the middle-class lifestyle.

One of the most telling ways they distinguished themselves was by using music to create an atmosphere of gentility in their homes and in their evening entertainment. As Lawrence Levine shows in his classic book *Highbrow/Lowbrow: The Emergence of Cultural Hierarchy in America*, it became increasingly important to well-to-do people in the post–Civil War United States to control the public settings in which they enjoyed music and other performing arts. Symphony music, opera, and theater were popular among working people before the Civil War. In fact, passions for Shakespeare ran so high among workers in New York that in 1849 about two dozen of them were killed in riots that broke out because of disputes with English critics over the ability of American actors to play Shakespearean characters. As the nineteenth century drew to a close, though, workers were squeezed out of theatrical and musical performances of the great works. When the wealthy and powerful built grand concert halls and theaters, the cost of admission became too high for workers to enjoy something they had once loved. Not surprisingly, many of them lost interest and moved on to other forms of entertainment.

Middle-class Americans participated to a degree in the increasingly expensive performing arts. But they also made their mark on the growing respectability and gentility of American musical culture by linking it with good manners, self-restraint, and other attributes of the Victorian era. Middle-class homes often featured parlors where well-brought-up young ladies and gentlemen played sentimental popular tunes on pianos, having taken lessons so they could read the sheet music for the latest ditty cranked out by tunesmiths who shaped the market as well as supplied it. Beginning in the 1880s, vast numbers of syrupy sweet love songs, odes to mother, and ballads encouraging good behavior came flowing out of the New York City songwriting district known as Tin Pan Alley. These songs and many more found their way to the parlors of the middle class. By the 1890s, middle-class Americans essentially had a stranglehold on the definition of good manners. They looked up to the wealthy captains of industry and down on the workers whose labor enriched the industrialists and made comfortable lives for many middle-income earners.

Their music was sweet but bland. They even disdained ragtime when it emerged in the 1890s, calling it shocking and lewd. Yet by the early twentieth century many middle-class families had acquired player pianos and piano rolls of ragtime pieces so they could enjoy them at home. Many people who played the piano found it difficult to play the rags, whose syncopation and complex interplay of left and right hands baffled many a player who had been brought up on classical piano literature. Once ragtime became acceptable to more people in the middle class, it began to seem hopelessly old-fashioned and quaint to others who wanted something more daring. When jazz erupted on the scene, defenders of ragtime denounced it as scurrilous—just as defenders of the parlor songs had denounced ragtime. Even in a city as tolerant of free living as New Orleans, even in the early 1900s, jazz was a shock to the system. Again, no one knows exactly what it sounded like before it began to be recorded in the late 1910s and early 1920s, but reports of eyewitnesses feature plentiful complaints and denunciations from the high-minded and self-righteous would-be arbiters of morality and decency.

It is pointless to speculate whether something sounding like jazz would later have emerged somewhere else if the peculiar mixture of influences and raw material had not been available in New Orleans. The facts are that they *were* available and that jazz arose there, with profound effects. New Orleans put its special stamp on the music that became jazz in the early twentieth century, and that stamp emphasized revolution, at least in the sense that it rejected Victorian manners and celebrated the free-spirited, libertine approach to life that came to be identified with the Jazz Age. The old impulses of squelching misbehavior did not go away just because jazz happened. In fact, anti-alcohol forces succeeded in making it illegal to manufacture or sell liquor in the United States during the early years of the twentieth century, something temperance activists had been advocating for more than a hundred years.

No one had foreseen, though, that the incredible economic growth made possible by the post–Civil War industrial boom would create two largely new phenomena: leisure and spending money. Young people born into middle-class families found a very different world from what their parents and grandparents had known. To a great extent, the industrial wealth of the United States in the late nineteenth and early twentieth centuries created the teenager. In the not-too-distant past, most twenty-year-olds could already have had ten years of full-time work experience. Children were seen by many employers, and by many parents, simply as small adults, undersized workers whose lot in life was to make money for their elders. They had little opportunity to grow up; they simply went to work. Child-labor laws helped alleviate some of this injustice, at least in most cities. But the chief factors that "created" adolescence as a transition period between childhood and adulthood were the availability of free time and of money to spend on ways to enjoy it. Many young people spent that money on jazz.

This is not to say that only young people enjoyed jazz when it first appeared, but to a great extent it was the music of the young and rebellious who enjoyed shocking their stuffy parents and who kept up with the latest trends in clothing, hairstyles, slang, and general misbehavior as well as music. They stayed out late and pumped vast amounts of money into the nightclubs and dance halls where jazz was remaking the cultural landscape of much of the United States. Not everyone participated in this upheaval. The same decades that saw the creation of jazz also saw the rise of religious fundamentalism, hysterical anti-radicalism, and Prohibition, the "great experiment" that created a vast empire of illegal enterprises dedicated to providing people with liquor, including nightclubs where jazz became popular. Those who reveled in jazz, however, delighted in upsetting the sensitivities of people who preferred to keep a lid on American popular culture, trying to put a genie back into a bottle that was already in pieces.

More difficult to grasp today is how different the music that grew into jazz sounded from one neighborhood to another in New Orleans. The music played in the Tremé neighborhood, for instance, a section just to the north and east of the French Quarter, was different from that played in the near-uptown neighborhood where Louis spent much of his time growing up. He moved around town, sampling the array of music available, making himself known to the musicians who produced it, and picking up ideas from everyone he heard in various musical neighborhoods. He also excelled

at playing in parades, an important musical tradition in New
Orleans and one of the ways musical styles from one neighborhood influenced players in other areas.

Marching bands were popular in many towns and cities
throughout the United States, but those in New Orleans
took on a style of their own. In other places the marching
bands usually played marches. As obvious as that seems, it
was an important contrast to the music played by the marching bands of New Orleans, which became famous for playing
popular tunes, even folk songs and hymns. They began moving away from the two-four time that so many marching
bands used. Two-four made it easier to march to something
like John Philip Sousa's classic march tune "Stars and Stripes
Forever." Sousa was enormously popular at the precise moment when jazz was rising. Vast numbers of jazz musicians,
especially drummers and brass players, received their basic
training in bands that played Sousa. In most places Sousa's
music was popular because marching was almost as much
about looking sharp going down the street as it was about
making interesting music. Staying in step was crucial. It was
marching, after all, not just walking while playing music,
that made two-four rhythm so important.

Marching bands that made their way through the neighborhoods of New Orleans were most interested in drawing
a crowd through their captivating sound. They had to compete for attention with an astonishing variety of musicians
and musical organizations. That required a powerful, energetic sound, preferably something different from what everyone else was playing. By the 1910s many marching bands
were playing ragtime, which had become popular and was
similar in rhythmic structure to marches. Thus it was relatively easy for bands to play while marching. Scott Joplin
even wrote a number of songs called "ragtime marches."
New Orleans bands played a great many rags in this period

and began putting their own special interpretation on ragtime. That helped set them apart not just from the bands of other cities but from the many musical offerings available in New Orleans. The street bands became especially noted for their appearances during Carnival parades leading up to and including Mardi Gras, and for playing in the famous "jazz funerals" that led mourners sorrowfully to the grave site of the deceased and then led them out in a raucous celebration of life that demonstrates the devil-may-care attitude of so many New Orleanians.

Armstrong's own description of a jazz funeral, in his book *Satchmo*, is worth retelling: "The funerals in New Orleans are sad until the body is finally lowered into the grave [or placed into an above-ground crypt in many water-logged neighborhoods] and the Reverend says, 'ashes to ashes and dust to dust.'" Then "the band would strike up one of those good old tunes like Didn't He Ramble, and all the people would leave their worries behind. . . . Once the band starts, everybody starts swaying from one side of the street to the other, especially those who drop in and follow the ones who have been to the funeral. These people are known as the 'second line' and they may be anyone passing along the street who wants to hear the music. The spirit hits them and they follow along to see what's happening."

Sometimes it seemed that the New Orleans marching bands were not marching but merely walking along. No one much cared; players and listeners were captivated by the replacement of the two-four ragtime beat with a four-four beat. No one knows who introduced this innovation, but it became one of the hallmarks of jazz. Four-four time gave musicians more freedom than two-four, because it allowed more room in each measure or portion of a song for musicians to "play with" the melody. They did not have to be as slavishly devoted to the alternating bass rhythm that was so characteristic of both march music and ragtime—though it is well to point out that some New Orleans musicians used the term "ragtime" to refer to any "hot" style of music in the pre-jazz era, whether it was played by a street band or some other group.

Pioneering jazz musicians were drawn to the syncopation of ragtime, but in time they were put off by its restrictions, its rhythmic straitjacket. The street bands, even if they were not exactly playing jazz, did something else that influenced Armstrong and many other early jazz players. They developed a practice of playing around the melody of a song. This gave each wind instrument a way to keep playing, even if it did not have the melody, but also did not require everyone who did not have the melody to play a predetermined line of harmony notes. A lead instrument, usually the cornet, would play the melody, but everyone was playing something, usually throughout the song. Many experts refer to this practice in New Orleans as "polyphony" because of the way several instruments drive the melody forward. But they weren't all playing the melody or playing a strict harmony pattern. They took turns playing, and playing around, the melody. This practice gave energy to the street bands, a high degree of satisfaction to the musicians, and a great deal of excitement to the people who listened to them play and watched them snap off down the street.

Many of the musicians from the street bands also played the dance halls that doubled as marketplaces for the services of prostitutes. Because these bands obviously did not have to march, they were freer to develop an even fresher sound than the marching bands. They moved the city's music further toward jazz, playing around a melody as the street bands did but also building more heavily on a foundation of blues songs. Prostitutes wanted the bands to play slow blues numbers so they could induce dance partners to move to the next level of commercial involvement in the evening's array of services. To keep a blues song interesting to five or six musicians while only one was playing the melody required a freedom for everyone in the band to play something new or flashy.

This was the musical scene Louis entered when, at the age of thirteen, he left the Waif's Home for the last time. It demanded the ability to make music in a variety of settings, especially those replete with prostitutes. As it turned out, he did pretty well. He thought of his own success with the prostitutes as coming from several advantages he had, as he says in *Satchmo:* "They all liked me because I was little and cute and I could play the kind of blues they liked. Whenever the gals had done good business they would come into the honky-tonk in the wee hours of the morning and walk right up to the bandstand. As soon as I saw them out of the corner of my eye I would tell Boogus, my piano man, and Garbee, my drummer man, to get set for a good tip. Then Boogus would go into some good old blues and the gals would scream with delight."

Hanging around the prostitutes and their places of business was not all fun and games. Louis saw many scary events unfold before his young eyes, especially some knife fights that never left his memory. He was once stabbed himself by a woman who wanted him to spend the night with her. Although he considered her his "chick," he told her he was too young to spend a night away from his mother's house. She took a dim view of that attitude and stuck him in the shoulder. He tried to hide the wound and the damage it did to his shirt. But his mother noticed, grilled him about the incident, and got herself over to the woman's house to tell her to leave her son alone. "The girl was just about ready to go to bed when Mayann banged on her door," Armstrong later recalled. "The minute she opened the door Mayann grabbed her by the throat" and said, "What you stab my son for?" Armstrong's mother threw her to the floor and began choking her. Armstrong believed she would have killed the woman if she had not been pulled off by a musician friend of his he called Black Benny. "Benny knew Mayann well, and he and I had played quite a few funerals together," Armstrong wrote. As fearsome as his mother's love was, the raw emotions and volatility of life in a society where life could be lost in an instant impressed Louis even more. Street life in New Orleans was, as he often said, "rough."

After he left the home, Louis solidified his reputation as an up-and-coming musical talent by performing in a variety of bands both in the honky-tonks and on the street. He loved playing the parades but, more important, won himself the opportunity to play in the better-known clubs and dance halls where for years he had been longing to perform. Yet he was not established enough to make a living as a full-time musician. Remarkably few people were able to do so in those days. For a while he went back to helping provide support for his family. To make additional money he took a variety of jobs doing manual labor, including delivering coal by driving a wagon pulled by a mule. In *Satchmo* he writes: "I worked on a junk wagon with a fellow named Lorenzo. He was a very funny fellow and he did not pay me much, but the fun we used to have going all over the city to collect rags, bones and bottles from the rich as well as the poor!" Lorenzo was also a music fan and played a little toy horn in ways that impressed young Louis. "When I was with him I was in my element," Armstrong writes. "The things he said about music held me spellbound, and he blew that old, beat-up tin horn with such warmth that I felt as though I was sitting with a good cornet player."

Louis was careful to treat his elders with respect. He had been taught to do so, and it often allowed him to play or sing with more experienced musicians and to work on his sense of professionalism as a musician. Lorenzo, for instance, had terrible teeth, something that mystified Louis. "With all the money he made he never got his teeth fixed. Every other tooth was missing, and he looked just like he was laughing twice as hard as anyone else when something funny was said. But I did not dare put him wise to this because I did not want older folks to think me a sassy child." His respectful attitude got him the chance to practice his singing, and his broad-minded views of music gave him a sense that enjoyment of the song was more important than the genre it represented: "There were many different kinds of people and instruments to inspire me to carry on with my music when I was a boy. I always loved music, and it did not matter what the instrument was or who played it so long as the playing was good. I used to hear some of the finest music in the world listening to the barroom quartets who hung around the saloons with a cold can of beer in their hands, singing up a breeze while they passed the can around. I thought I was really somebody when I got so I could hang around with those fellows and sing and drink out of the can with them. When I was a teen-ager those old-timers let me sing with them and carry the lead, bless their hearts. Even in those days they thought I had something on the ball as a ragtime singer, which is what hot swing singing is today."

As satisfying as such experiences were for Louis, most of his teen years were spent trying to eke out a living. In 1918 he also married a young prostitute, Daisy Parker, whom he had met at a club in one of the New Orleans suburbs, Gretna, on the West Bank, across the Mississippi River from the main part of the city. She was twenty-one years old; he was still a teenager. Daisy worked at a place called the Brick House, which Armstrong says in *Satchmo* "was one of the toughest joints I ever played in. It was the honky-tonk where levee workers would congregate every Saturday night and trade with the gals who'd stroll up and down the floor and into the bar. Those guys would drink and fight one another like circle saws. Bottles would come flying over the bandstand like crazy, and there was lots of just plain common shooting and cutting. But somehow all of that jive didn't faze me at all. I was so happy to have some place to blow my horn." In keeping with the place where they met, Louis and his bride had a turbulent relationship and separated soon after their marriage, though it lasted for several years. More important for his budding career, he earned a reputation as a hardworking, energetic musician who was easy to get along with. He played with several groups, including the Tuxedo Brass Band, and caught the ear of more established musicians like Kid Ory.

Ory and Joe Oliver, Armstrong's hero, led one of the best New Orleans bands. But Oliver moved to Chicago in 1918 as part of the "great migration" of Southern blacks in the World War I era and after. They moved north in great numbers, drawn by the hope of better jobs, by opportunities they thought the war might produce, and to escape the constant restraints they faced in the Jim Crow South. The South had no monopoly on racial prejudice and legal segregation, which existed in many places outside the region. But their power was less overt in the North, less dangerous than in the South, less destructive to the soul. Louis knew his time to leave was coming, in part because so many other New Orleans musicians, including Joe Oliver, were leaving in the wake of police harassment for being associated with the city's rough nightlife. This helped Louis get jobs in other places, however, because so many musicians had left the city. His reputation was growing, but it was strongest within a small circle of observant older players. He was helped by the fact that his talent was matched by his likability. His pleasant manner and infectious enthusiasm earned him many friends who helped him find his way through the pitfalls of New Orleans life.

When Kid Ory hired Louis to take the place of the great Oliver, Armstrong leaped to the top ranks of young instrumentalists in the heady, competitive world of New Orleans music. He had immense power with his cornet for such a young player. But he also played with quality, not just volume. He was on his way, and he knew what this would mean on the street level and what the opportunity represented.

Armstrong recalls that at first he had a hard time believing his good fortune. Ory told him later that when some of the men in his band suggested he get Armstrong to take Oliver's place, "He was a little in doubt at first, but after he'd looked around the town he decided I was the right one to have a try at taking that great man's place. . . . What a thrill that was! To think I was considered up to taking Joe Oliver's place in the best band in town."

Playing with Ory exposed Louis to new aspects of the musician's life, especially glimpses into the worlds of privilege that the top bands moved in and out of and the snobbery they sometimes had to deal with. In *Satchmo* he recalls that "Kid Ory had some of the finest gigs, especially for the rich white folks. Whenever we'd play a swell place, such as the Country Club, we would get more money, and during the intermissions the people giving the dance would see that the band had a big delicious meal, the same as they ate. And by and by the drummer and I would get in with the colored waiters and have enough food to take home to Mayann and Mama Lucy.

"The music-reading musicians like those in [Creole orchestra leader John Robichaux's] band thought that we in Kid Ory's band were good, but only good together. One day those big shots had a funeral to play, but most of them were working during the day and couldn't make it. So they engaged most of Ory's boys, including me. The day of the funeral the musicians were congregating at the hall where the Lodge started their march, to go up to the dead brother's house. Kid Ory and I noticed all those stuck-up guys giving us lots of ice. They didn't feel we were good enough to play their marches." Once the playing started, Ory's band members did pretty well, finding the music easier to play than they thought it would be. "Then they brought the body out of the house and we went on to the cemetery. After we reached the cemetery, and they lowered the body down six feet in the ground, and the drummer man rolled on the drums, they struck a ragtime march which required swinging from the band. And those old fossils just couldn't cut it. That's when we Ory boys took over and came in with flying colors."

They went on playing, working the people in the second line into a frenzy: "We went into the hall swinging the last number, *Panama*. I remembered how Joe Oliver used to swing that last chorus in the upper register, and I went on up there and got those notes, and the crowd went wild." The reaction of the music lovers was one thing, but the reaction of the other musicians was worth even more to Louis: "After that incident those stuck-up guys wouldn't let us alone. . . . They hired us several times afterward. After all, we'd proved to them that any learned musician can read music, but they can't all swing. It was a good lesson for them."

Ory's band did not play every night, but it played often enough that Louis got a good deal of exposure and soon had offers to leave New Orleans for larger opportunities. Ory himself moved to Los Angeles in 1919 and invited Armstrong to join him there, to satisfy the growing market for the new music. Louis was not keen to move to Los Angeles, but he continued to think about leaving and did so, at least on a limited basis, when he decided to take a job on a steamboat.

Fate Marable's Orchestra aboard the steamer *Capitol*, circa 1920. Steamboat travel on the Mississippi was mostly a novelty by the time Armstrong got a job playing in Marable's band, but he used the experience to hone his professional skills.

One of the owners of a steamboat that hired musicians heard Louis playing with Ory's band and offered him a job on a Mississippi riverboat. Although steamers had lost out to trains as a major mode of transportation, they continued to take tourist excursions up and down the river and had a long record even then of keeping musicians on board. The Streckfus family of St. Louis owned the steamboat line that Louis went to work for. Captain Joseph Streckfus had been putting black musicians on his boats for several years, providing his passengers with both a proto-jazz band and a more sedate foxtrot orchestra for listening and dancing. The band Armstrong joined was led by an African-American pianist named Fate Marable, and it played the jazzlike music. It became so popular that Captain Streckfus let the foxtrot orchestra go.

It was perhaps fitting that a man named Fate used that most powerful symbol of New Orleans' importance to the nation—the river—to get Louis Armstrong out of the city, something he grew more aware that he badly needed to do. The opportunity to play with Marable provided him with several crucial experiences. It constituted something of an apprenticeship, filling several key gaps in his musical education. He always said there was no question that it helped him improve his musicianship. For one thing, Marable and a couple of his band members, David Jones and Joe Howard, worked with Louis on his ability to read and interpret sheet music. He started work on the boats with the barest rudimentary knowledge of formal music and ended his time there with a foundational ability to read sheet music that carried him through the rest of his career. Jones helped him particularly, turning Louis away from being what the old musicians called a "speller," someone who could look at a piece of sheet music and pick out the notes by counting up E-G-B-D-F and F-A-C-E on the lines and spaces of the treble clef but who could not sight read.

Louis's ability to pick up tunes by ear helped him. He was quick. But Marable required more. Armstrong writes in *Satchmo*: "Fate knew all this when he hired me, but he liked my tone and the way I could catch on. That was enough for him." Marable had confidence that being around experienced musicians would help Louis improve his musicianship, and he was correct. Louis was indeed a quick study, and before long he was able to play anything Marable put in front of him. But Marable never let up and constantly worked to keep the men in his band on their toes. He had a habit of memorizing his own part in a new piece of music while the others were taking a break, then, "After running his part down to perfection he would stamp his foot and say: 'O.K. men. Here's your parts.'. . . Then we all scrambled to read the tune at first sight. By the time we were able to play our parts Fate had learned to play his without the [written] notes. I thought that was marvelous."

Marable the taskmaster made a lasting impression on Louis. If one of the musicians made a serious mistake, Marable would wait until it seemed that no one, including the leader, had noticed the problem. Then, "When you came to work the next day with a bad hangover from the night before, he picked up the music you had failed with and asked you to play it before the other members of the band. And believe me, brother, it was no fun to be shown up before all the other fellows if you did not play that passage right; we used to call this experience our Waterloo. This was Fate's way of making his men rest properly so that they could work perfectly on the job the next night. I learned something from that."

Playing with Marable was an extraordinarily valuable experience for the young Armstrong in other ways as well. For one thing, he had regular work every day, and the discipline that having to play every night brought with it. Also, because not only Marable but also the Streckfus family had high standards, Louis had to keep improving his musicianship to be able to hold his job. That meant playing with the other musicians and keeping up with them, not just playing at the same time they were playing. He also had the benefit of being around a great deal of talent. The band featured a remarkable lineup of excellent players, many of New Orleans origins, including the Dodds brothers—Johnny and "Baby" (Warren)—Johnny St. Cyr, George "Pops" Foster, George Brashear, Henry "Red" Allen, and Honore Dutrey.

Playing with Marable made Louis known to a wider variety of musicians who went on to achieve great things in the jazz world, including white musicians such as Bix Beiderbecke, who recalled that he first heard Armstrong when Streckfus's steamboat docked in Beiderbecke's hometown of Davenport, Iowa. Playing with Marable also gave Louis an awareness of the audience for this new music outside New

Orleans, even in towns that lacked the free-spirited nature of his hometown. The first recordings of what could be called jazz were made only in 1917, and the music was still so new that its name was still a subject of some debate. Those first recordings were by the Original Dixieland "Jass" Band. Music very much like that of the ODJB was being played in several cities around the country, but Louis had little knowledge of that development. Traveling the Mississippi opened his eyes to a wider reality.

One of those realities was the possibility that music might bridge the social gulf that usually existed between the races in the United States. Armstrong always praised Marable for many things, including his contributions to spreading that previously unthinkable notion. Louis gave Marable credit for breaking down at least some of the racial barriers in towns along the Mississippi. In most of the towns where they stopped to play, especially the smaller ones, they were the first African-American musicians the townspeople had ever seen. In *Satchmo* he writes, "At first we ran into some ugly experiences while we were on the bandstand, and we had to listen to plenty of nasty remarks. But most of us were from the South anyway. We were used to that kind of jive, and we would just keep on swinging as though nothing had happened. Before the evening was over they *loved* us. We couldn't turn for them singing our praises and begging us to hurry back."

Playing with Marable gave Louis a clearer perspective on life in New Orleans. He was well aware of the social and economic inequities imbedded in the city's tangled race relations, seeing firsthand how skin color, including the color gradations of African Americans, could determine one's lot in life. Many New Orleans blacks endured the humiliation and degradation of the Jim Crow South. Powerful whites controlled the law, and the law restricted where African

Americans could go, how they got there, and what they did when they arrived. Something else altogether was the way blacks treated one another. For instance, black theater managers in New Orleans would use the "paper bag test" to decide if they would allow African Americans to enter the main level of their theaters. Black ticket buyers with fair skin would be allowed to take their seats on the main level while with those with skin darker than the color of a paper bag would be shunted to the balcony. These realities had deep roots in the complicated racial history of New Orleans, which included countless stories of free blacks who owned black slaves, Creoles of color who amassed fortunes and political influence and kept poor blacks as servants, and black mistresses who bore the children of white businessmen and civic leaders and prospered or floundered largely on the whims of their powerful paramours. Louis witnessed and experienced such behavior at the hands of other black New Orleanians, and bitterly disliked it.

In many ways New Orleans had been good to him. But it also represented a box he knew he needed to escape. Many African Americans were busy trying to get out of such boxes, including considerable numbers from New Orleans. When they went, like immigrants everywhere and always, they took as much of their culture with them as they could. This was one of the principal ways jazz spread to other parts of the country, and Louis Armstrong was one of the people who spread it.

He played with Marable's band for several seasons, finishing his last trip at the end of the summer of 1921. He had continued to play in bands in New Orleans between excursions, and turned down another invitation in the spring of 1922 to join a band the jazz pianist Fletcher Henderson was planning to organize in New York. Later that year, however, he jumped at the chance to leave when Joe Oliver invited him to come to Chicago to join his band. "On the afternoon of August 8," Gary Giddins writes, "he played a funeral with the Tuxedo Jazz Band, packed a small bag, including a trout sandwich his mother had fixed, and caught the evening train." He was twenty-one years old.

*

Armstrong's life represented a level of success that many African Americans held up as the pinnacle of full participation in the American dream narrative. He started on the same level where many of them started, and even lower than many—in abject poverty on the streets of New Orleans. His childhood—poor family, time spent in the Colored Waif's Home, vagabond existence on the streets of New Orleans—gave him a determination to succeed. This was reinforced by his experiences with other, more affluent African Americans in his native city and a desire to reflect well on those like him who had come from similarly humble beginnings. Louis's musical gifts gave him a way to make something of a living in New Orleans and a way to get out of the city. His life paralleled those of so many twentieth-century Southern blacks who realized their potential only when they escaped the South and came into their own in the North.

But Louis's growing up in New Orleans was essential to his success, even if he had to get away from the city to make an independent life for himself. Its extraordinarily rich musical landscape nurtured the jazz revolution, and he gladly felt himself swept along with its rising tide. But New Orleans was not just a jazz town. It embraced many different kinds of music—sung, played, listened to, danced to, talked about, bought, and sold. Louis loved just about all of it, tried his hand at several kinds, and never forgot one of the central lessons the music of New Orleans taught him—that an audience's ability to enjoy a song often had little to do with what kind of song it was. Coming up as a player in New Orleans also gave him a work ethic that served him well for the rest of his life and distinguished his career from those of many other fine musicians who faded from the scene because they were unwilling to work as hard as Armstrong did. Of course, few others had his talent. In that respect he had a clear advantage. But many other musicians could have benefited from Armstrong's dedication to his music and his work ethic.

New Orleans gave him something else that served him for the rest of his life: it showed him the foolishness of racism. The city scarcely had a monopoly on that particular sickness, but its peculiar ways of exhibiting racism gave him a keen sense of its injustice. It also gave him a clear understanding of the limits of what one individual could do to combat the pernicious and all-pervasive social systems that grew out of racism. Many of Armstrong's fellow black New Orleanians succumbed to the hatred that racism engendered. They lashed out, were punished, and disappeared before the might of the Jim Crow system and its legal structures. For whatever reason, Armstrong was able to keep in check that tendency to hate. Possibly this ability came from his music—the love of creativity, the sweet sensation of providing an audience with pleasing sounds and happy moments. Perhaps it was just his preference for happiness over controversy. He spoke out against racism and segregation later in his career, not as often as some would have wanted. But when he did, he spoke out in his own way, as he did in his music.

All these attributes, skills, and perceptions served him well as he headed north to pursue his own musical and professional path.

CHAPTER THREE

Hot Music in a Strange Time

🎜 Louis Armstrong's early life paralleled almost exactly the rise of jazz and the development of the recording industry that helped make jazz and other forms of "race" music highly lucrative features of the entertainment marketplace in twentieth-century America. New Orleans jazz musicians felt the pull of Northern money and the higher degree of freedom they could experience away from the Jim Crow South. As so many African Americans did in the years after World War I, in 1922 Armstrong headed for Chicago.

It was a strange time. The post–World War I era featured mixtures of liberation and repression. Sometime during the war, the population of the United States shifted from a rural to an urban majority, bringing an increasingly educated and, many said, enlightened citizenry. But fundamentalism also captivated many throughout the country, North as well as South. Women had gained the vote in a presidential election for the first time in 1920 and were joining the workforce in growing numbers. Yet conventional thinking brought hopes that the country could return to some imaginary golden age of small-town purity, which many people thought they heard in the reassuring terms of the mediocre president they helped elect in 1920. Warren Harding coined the term "normalcy" to describe the state he hoped the country would regain after two decades of progressive reform and a strenuous

Armstrong, standing, with Joe Oliver, his mentor, sometime sur-
rogate father, and hero, dating to their common time in New Orleans. This formal portrait was taken in Chicago, shortly after Oliver brought Armstrong to join his band there. *(Photograph by Mrs.
Mona MacMurray)*

war that his predecessor, President Woodrow Wilson, had
labeled a crusade to preserve the very foundations of Western civilization. Harding thought the country needed to give
all this frenzied effort a rest and get back to the old ways of
being and doing. Jazz musicians, however, had other plans.
Armstrong was one of them, which is one of the reasons he
joined a group of fellow New Orleans musicians led by King
Oliver, the Creole Jazz Band. They took Chicago by storm.

Oliver's prime venue was the Lincoln Gardens Café on Chicago's South Side, where his principal task was to provide music for dancing. Since World War II few people have thought of jazz as dance music; from the 1950s onward it has been the musical equivalent of a spectator sport. But in the 1920s dancing was the rage, and jazz was the music for dancing. Ragtime had helped make the musical transition from listening to dancing, from sitting around the piano in the parlor to dancing to a piano in a tavern or a bordello, and New Orleans had offered plenty of venues for participation. Most of the dancing in those places had been slow "drags," which dance partners did in contact with each other to songs with lilting, fairly slow tempos. In the 1920s, however, dancing became more athletic, still requiring a partner but sometimes performed without even touching one's partner. Oliver's band seldom played at breakneck speed, catering to the bunny hug and foxtrots that were impossible to perform at too fast a tempo. Oliver's band consisted mostly of New Orleans players he had known back home, and they were plenty good. When Armstrong arrived and heard the band for the first time, he was a bit intimidated. He thought they were so good that he might not be able to find a place among them. The next night, however, he played with the band for the first time. The performance was so successful, in large part because of Oliver's special efforts to make Armstrong welcome, that Armstrong felt at home.

Armstrong's own description of his first night in Oliver's band shows his deep appreciation for Oliver's sponsorship and his awareness that getting to Chicago signaled the real beginning of his career as a musician. In *Satchmo* he writes, "Every number on opening night was a gassuh." A special number they performed was called "Eccentric." Oliver would play a four-bar section, then the band would do the same, going back and forth. "Finally at the very last chorus Joe and Bill Johnson would do a sort of musical act. Joe would make his horn sound like a baby crying, and Bill Johnson would make his horn sound as though it was a nurse calming the baby in a high voice. While Joe's horn was crying, Bill Johnson's horn would interrupt on that high note as though to say, 'Don't cry, little baby.'" Finally this musical horseplay broke up in a wild squabble between nurse and child, and the number would bring down the house with laughter and applause.

After the floor show the band played a number of dance tunes, and people in the crowd began to yell, "Let the youngster blow!" Armstrong writes in *Satchmo*, "That meant me. Joe was wonderful and he gladly let me play my rendition of the blues. That was heaven." Oliver was pleased with the crowd's reaction and played a half-hour longer than planned. Backstage the band received congratulations from admirers, including other musicians who had seen the show and now praised Oliver for having such a good band and for having gotten Armstrong to join it. "I was so happy I did not know what to do," Armstrong recalled. "I had hit the big time. I was up North with the greats. I was playing with my idol, the King, Joe Oliver. My boyhood dream had come true at last."

Armstrong admired Oliver's musical ability, but he also knew that Oliver would watch out for him in the new city. It was one thing to run up and down the Mississippi on a riverboat out of New Orleans. No matter how disagreeable certain aspects of the trip might be—and the cranky Fate Marable and the demanding Streckfus family could be a chore—there was always an endpoint to a steamboat excursion. Moving to Chicago, on the other hand, was a break with New Orleans. It meant a great deal to Armstrong that

Oliver would be there, and he looked forward to having the great bandleader in his life, perhaps not as a father figure but at least as a big brother.

Chicago was a departure from New Orleans in another sense: its business culture was a great deal more intense, and it was closely related to its crime subculture. There had been crime in New Orleans, of course. Armstrong had participated in minor illegal activities and knew which people to avoid and how to stay out of serious trouble. But Chicago crime was different because Chicago was different. The people of Chicago thought of themselves as masters of the American future, at least the part of it that involved the area between the Atlantic and Pacific coasts. The city felt new. Because of the Great Fire of 1871, a great deal of it was in fact new. New Orleans had been old, established, colonial. That had not kept the city from being the birthplace of jazz.

But in New Orleans, music existed primarily to provide entertainment. In Chicago it seemed to exist to make money. The differences in the two approaches to music were as different as the cities were from each other. About the only thing they had in common was jazz. This had special meaning because of the extent of gang dominance of commerce in Chicago. There was no way to be involved in the entertainment business there and avoid a connection with organized crime. More important for Armstrong, the view of music as a business remained at least in the back of his mind, a legacy of his time in Chicago.

Armstrong had plenty of fun in Chicago. It certainly was not all business. He told of going to hear a fine New Orleans–born cornet player named Freddie Keppard play. Oliver's piano player, Memphis native Lil Hardin, would play with Keppard's band after getting off work with Oliver's group, and she took Armstrong with her one night. He says in *Louis Armstrong, in His Own Words*, that Keppard had a habit of setting up on the front left side of the bandstand so he could make himself heard and be able to kid the customers on their way to and from the restrooms. "And Freddie had a lot of fun greeting his friends, disciples, etc. I laughed until I cried when Freddie—just before he started to play a tune—a real cute, pretty little Blonde Ofay (white) Chick walked by the bandstand coming from the ladies rest room. Freddie spoke to her real, Cute. 'Oh, Hello,' he said in a real high voice. And the cute little Chick smiled and said HELLO in a Real heavy voice. And it tickled everybody too much until even Freddie—laughed out loud—and almost fell off the bandstand."

Lincoln Gardens played a crucial role in redefining "home" for jazz musicians, Armstrong included. According to Collier, it was "probably the most celebrated band location in jazz history, for it was here that the Northern musicians and the early jazz fans of both races began to acquire the true faith." The Gardens was a white-owned club with a black clientele, frequent visits from white customers, and, from time to time, a designated whites-only night. But it was one of the most important places in the United States where jazz demonstrated that it was on its way to becoming a national phenomenon, not just a fad and not just something peculiar to New Orleans and its refugees.

One of the great events in Armstrong's career occurred soon after his arrival in Chicago: he was introduced to the artistry and stagecraft of the great dancer Bill "Bojangles" Robinson. Armstrong recalled in 1970 how powerful an effect seeing Robinson had on him in 1922. He admired Robinson immediately and always remembered the extraordinary effect the man's stage presence had on any audience. Forty-eight years later Armstrong still recalled everything about that 1922 performance, even the clothes Robinson wore. In *Louis Armstrong, in His Own Words*, he tells how

he first saw Robinson perform: "I had [bass player] Bill Johnson take me to see a matinee show one day so I could see
this man whom I had heard and read about in my early days
in N.O. And Bojangles came up to every expectation and
opinion that I had of him before I saw him in person. I am
sitting in my seat in the theater very anxious to see this
man. And sure enough the great one appeared. As he came
out of the wing on stage the first thing that hit him was the
Flashlight. Sharp—Lord know that man was so Sharp he was
Bleeding (our expression when we mention someone who's
well dressed). Anyway, he had on a sharp light tan Gabardine
summer suit, Brown Derby and the usual expensive thick
[-soled] shoes in which he taps in.

"It was a long time before Bojangles could open his mouth.
That's how popular he was and well liked by all who understood his greatness as a dancer and a showman. He waited
after the Thunderous Applause had finished—And looked
up into the booth and said to the man who controlled the
lights—Bill said to him 'Give me a light my color.' And all
the lights all over the house went out. And me sitting there
when this happened with the whole audience just Roaring
with laughter. . . . I was Laughing so loud until Bill Johnson
whom I was with was on a verge of taking me out of there.
I hadn't heard anything like that before or witnessed it either. Then Bojangles went into his act. His every move was
a beautiful picture. I am sitting in my seat in thrilled ecstasy
and delight, even in a trance. He imitated a Trombone with
his walking cane to his mouth, blowing out of the side of his
mouth making the buzzing sound of a trombone, which I enjoyed. He told a lot of Funny jokes, which everybody enjoyed
immensely. Then he went into his dance and finished by
skating off of the stage with a silent sound and tempo. Wow
what an artist. I was sold on him ever since."

Armstrong took to life in Chicago and settled in happily
to his routine as a member of the Creole Jazz Band, hop-

Joseph "King" Oliver's band, shown here in 1924, featured some of the great jazz musicians of the 1920s. From left, Charlie Jackson, Clifford "Snag" Jones, William "Buster" Bailey, Joe Oliver, Alvin "Zue" Robertson, Lil Hardin Armstrong, Louis Armstrong, Rudy Jackson. *(Photograph by Duncan Schiedt)*

ing for the day when he would have the kind of effect on an audience that Bojangles Robinson had. Oliver worked his musicians pretty hard, but the immediate and huge success they enjoyed balanced out the demands of playing every night and rehearsing much of every day. After a while, Oliver had his band making recordings, which they did off and on for most of 1923. Although Chicago was moving to establish itself as a recording center for musicians throughout the central United States, the Creole Jazz Band's first recordings were made for the Gennett Record Company of Richmond, Indiana.

One could hardly describe the settings where recordings were made in those days as "studios," but Richmond became a prominent recording venue for a remarkable variety of artists representing a number of styles. The Gennett

Company attracted some of the most important figures in American popular music, and created what is generally recognized as the first great body of recorded jazz music. This work became the starting point for a great many musicians who learned from it, copied it, elaborated on it, and finally departed from it. The work put its stamp on jazz and on its growing numbers of fans. The Gennett recordings thus helped shape the new music that was overturning the timeworn Victorian sentimentality that had dominated American popular culture.

Despite this momentous role in the history of recorded music, the Gennett Company offered an unadorned experience for those musicians seeking to immortalize themselves on wax disks. As a matter of fact, Laurence Bergreen writes, "The Gennett recording facilities were as hostile to musicians as Richmond's social climate was to blacks. It would be hard to imagine a worse place to record music." Years before a time when musicians would be pampered and fawned over at recording sessions, they had to maintain a stoic determination just to survive the experience. And they had to approach the session concentrating on creating something worth saving, something worth selling. The commercial possibilities of the still-new recording industry were beginning to dawn on entrepreneurs and everyone else in the production line, from composer to purchaser. By the time the Creole Jazz Band made its first recordings in 1923, the industry had about a decade of general production experience, and blues performers had already demonstrated the huge sales potential of "race" music. This meant that white people, who were more likely to be able to afford the cumbersome and expensive phonograph machines, had to be willing to buy recordings of black musicians. African-American customers bought a great many records too, it turned out. But the great blues singer Mamie Smith showed that whites and blacks both would buy them when in 1920 she made a hit recording of the "Crazy Blues."

It took two years more for jazz recordings to begin to flow, and the recordings were still produced in somewhat primitive surroundings, as they were for several more years. Often recording engineers simply set up their equipment in large rooms in warehouses—or anyplace where a band could spread out but still be able to gather around the one horn, or later the microphone, that collected the entirety of the sound. Balancing this sound was often difficult; the equipment was temperamental and sensitive. Drummers often had to muffle various parts of their kits to keep from overwhelming the other instruments. Particularly powerful instrumentalists might have to move away from the point where the sound was collected. Armstrong's sound was so strong that it is said he occasionally had to stand many feet back from the machine. The whole experience created an odd, staggered effect for musicians accustomed to performing on a stage, in a line, facing an audience or a room filled with dancers. Playing in a circle, with certain players farther from the microphone than others, proved awkward for many musicians in recording sessions in the 1920s. As Bergreen writes, "without an audience, without booze, without time to rehearse," they had to play shortened versions of their songs, choking off most of the improvisational energy and joy that characterized their live performances. Bergreen suggests that recording particularly cramped Armstrong's style because "the length of his wild solos surpassed the capacity of wax cylinders and early records."

Added to these obstacles was a natural suspiciousness about recording held by many pioneering jazz musicians. They believed the record companies were out to take advantage of their music, which was certainly true, and that recordings would ruin people's interest in paying to see the bands in person—though this was rarely the case. The recording companies paid musicians a tiny sum for a full day's work, then made vast sums of money from sales of the records. But Oliver and his band, especially Armstrong, made the most of a tricky situation, as one can tell by listening to the music they recorded in 1923. Even with all the restrictions and limitations of the recording technology of the day, and even as exciting as it was to see and hear the band live, these recordings became the foundation of Armstrong's fame as a jazz musician, even more than the legendary Chicago performances.

The music that the Creole Jazz Band recorded in Richmond reveals several important features of early jazz. First, though the band was based in Chicago and picked up a great many ideas from other players there, they demonstrated most powerfully their deep roots in New Orleans. The birthplace of jazz created an ebullient, even boisterous music that epitomized the spirit of rebellious joy. Songs were held together by the rhythm section, usually drums and banjo but sometimes also an upright bass or guitar. And to a great extent, in early jazz the piano was considered a rhythm instrument. Oliver instructed Lil Hardin to play strong chords as backing to the essential beat of the song—up-and-down music with her hands and arms, not left-to-right music with her fingers. When she played delicate little runs, Oliver would scowl at her and mutter, "We already got a clarinet in the band." The drumming traditions of New Orleans often gave jazz a distinct feel very different from that of later music. That is, instead of alternating beats the way many drummers did and still do—one strike on a snare drum trading beats with the bass drum, for instance—many drummers in the New Orleans style kept up a steady pattern on the snare drum, most often with both hands. This style is believed to have its origins in the military bands that appeared often in New

Orleans during the formative years leading to the creation of jazz and in stories of Native American drumming that had captivated African Americans from slavery times. The other rhythm instruments kept up a straight line of beats but changed chords or single notes on virtually every beat, giving the music a powerful sense of forward motion.

Each song had a melody, of course, for popular music in the early twentieth century, even jazz, was not so revolutionary that it could depart from the notion that someone who liked a song should be able to hum or whistle its basic tune. But in New Orleans jazz that melody was elaborated by an amazing series of variations on the song's "theme," by which the entire soundscape was filled with strings of notes. The cornet nearly always played the melody line, and the trombone, saxophone, clarinet, and occasionally tuba would provide the polyphony. The musicians had to be highly disciplined to be able to tear through a fast song and not get in the way of the melody, or perform the slower pieces with sufficient sensitivity to the pacing and balance that kept a slow song delicate without sounding droopy. They also had to be able to get through often complicated arrangements without sounding stiff or overly rehearsed. The trick was to sound spontaneous rather than chaotic, skilled rather than rigid. Arrangements were usually worked out well in advance of a performance or recording session, often requiring the musicians to set out their notes on paper—in contrast to the impression many people have that jazz musicians were unable to read music.

But the next step in the process was essential. The musicians had to memorize the arrangements—which instrument took the melody, which ones played which variations, how the harmonies would work—and be able to reproduce the arrangements on stage, frequently under trying conditions. A musician could not afford to be distracted by the setting, by what was going on in a dance hall or nightclub; keeping these arrangements straight in one's head proved to be the undoing of many a promising player. The "head" arrangements of Oliver's band showed a group that could keep all their roles sorted out while the team concept remained foremost in everyone's mind. Oliver was the star, but even he seldom stood out, as jazz at that moment was at heart an ensemble affair.

Armstrong played second cornet to Oliver's lead, and some of the duets they performed in their 1923 recordings became the stuff of legend. Especially on their "breaks"—passages in the progress of a song when everyone in the band would stop playing except for Oliver and Armstrong—the duets they worked out caused many a brass player headaches and heartaches trying to master the patterns and riffs that the two men put on those wax disks.

Armstrong felt a tremendous affinity with Oliver, a sense of ease that enabled the two to complement each other's playing and seemingly to read each other's minds when they played. Speaking in 1954, Armstrong said there was glory to be had in the bands of the 1920s, and in King Oliver's band it belonged to Oliver: "Joe Oliver and I developed a little system whereby we didn't have to write down the duet breaks—I was so wrapped up in him and lived his music that I could take second to his lead in a split second. That was just how much I lived his music. No one could understand how we did it, but it was easy. . . . I never tried to go over him, because Papa Joe was the man and I felt any glory that should come to me must go to him—I wanted him to have all the praise. To me Joe Oliver blew enough Horn for the both of us."

Hoagy Carmichael, a white piano player and songwriter who went on to become a great success, came to see the band with Bix Beiderbecke, the kid from Davenport, Iowa, who had heard Armstrong when he was touring on the Mississippi. Beiderbecke was something of a rarity among white jazz musicians. He was one whom the black jazz musicians wanted to hear. Armstrong was one of those black musicians, but at Lincoln Gardens Beiderbecke was there not to be heard but to satisfy his desire to hear Louis Armstrong. The two trumpeters admired each other, but it was clear that Beiderbecke was there to learn. Carmichael, on the other hand, was almost paralyzed with admiration. After one particularly rapturous solo by Armstrong, Carmichael said he thought to himself, "Why isn't everybody in the world here to hear that? . . . Something as unutterably stirring as that deserved to be heard by the world."

Armstrong worked marvelously well in this system of constant mutual support that permitted no one instrument, even the leader's, to stand out. But the time was coming when he would need to assert his independence from Oliver's stern leadership and, indeed, from the ensemble orientation of jazz. One of the keys to his transformation was his evolving relationship with Oliver's piano player, Lillian Hardin. Unlike Armstrong, Hardin had studied music formally over a period of several years and had attended college. Like Armstrong, she longed to depart an unhappy first marriage and saw in Louis his great potential for stardom. Most of the male musicians in Chicago, including everyone in Oliver's band, wanted to romance Hardin, but she rejected everyone except Armstrong. They obtained divorces from their spouses and married early in 1924.

Almost immediately Hardin began encouraging Armstrong to step out of Oliver's shadow and seek the spotlight. Partly with her encouragement, he decided to leave the Creole Jazz Band. He was reluctant to do so, and never lost his admiration for Oliver and his appreciation for the King's mentoring. But the band seemed to be in a state of transition.

Some members were unhappy, as often happens in groups of talented musicians with strong egos and a burning desire for time in the spotlight. Several players were leaving the band. It seemed to be a good time to pull away, chiefly because Armstrong knew he had more to offer than he would ever have a chance to show with Oliver. With Lil Hardin's help, he mustered the courage to leave. After being turned down by a couple of bands, he got a brief job playing with another band in Chicago. Then, in the fall of 1924, he went to work in New York City with Fletcher Henderson, who had long wanted Armstrong to play with his band.

To say that Armstrong electrified the entertainment scene in New York would be an understatement. Gary Giddins observes, "He taught New York to swing." His transition to working with Henderson was not without its rough spots, however. Chicago was a city whose musicians included vast numbers of Southern blacks. Many of them were gifted, trained performers, but few of them made fun of recent arrivals from the South. They had experienced plenty of hard living in the South and in Chicago. In New York, though, Armstrong's relatively unsophisticated manners, rough speaking style, lack of knowledge of the fine points of music, and general absence of understanding of the way truly big cities functioned made him the butt of many jokes by members of Henderson's band. Most of them were from the North, and several had significant college experience. They thought of themselves as members of the African-American elite, which in many ways they were. Lil Hardin too had found Armstrong's unsophisticated qualities unappealing, and she worked hard to improve his professional behavior and presentation, even his dress. But his treatment by the members of Henderson's band gave him a jolt.

Armstrong later described his apprehensions upon joining what he called a "big band." "Now that was [a] great moment of my life," he says in *Louis Armstrong, in His*

Own Words. "I arrived in New York on the day Fletcher was having rehearsal—And I was rather nervous when I walked into the place. Shook hands with 'Smack'—That's the name I later learned they all called Fletcher Henderson. He was very nice to me. And he could see I was a wee bit Frightened etc., his Band being the first Big time Orchestra I had the pleasure of joining."

Henderson decided to play around a bit and see how Armstrong, whom he had courted for so long, would react to joining his band. "Fletcher said to me—'So you're Louis Armstrong?'—I said 'yassuh.' He gave me a Cute little Smile of Approval and said—'Your part is up on the band stand.' I said 'yassuh' in my little Bashful way—and Away I went up to the stand. Now when I gotten on the stand—to my Chair—I notice that every thing was so quiet, etc.—Just like Musicians—when a new man joins a Band, the other Players doesn't have much to say to the New Man.—It looks like they were all waiting to see what I was going to do—They were figuring on me—And I was doing the same thing by them. . . . I had the 3rd Trumpet part—And was Thrilled at playing a part in such an All Star Band as Fletcher Henderson's band. Finally I Cut Loose one night while we were down at the Roseland Ballroom and all of the Band Boys just couldn't play for watching me."

As had happened with Lil, Armstrong's endearing personality and sheer greatness as an instrumentalist won over the scoffers in Henderson's band. Before long, their ridicule turned to admiration, then to earnest attempts to copy Louis's style. His passionate, bluesy playing contrasted so dramatically with the careful, often unimaginative performances of so many other New York musicians that he literally ushered in a new era in jazz.

To appreciate how remarkable was his effect on the New York music scene, it should be noted that even in New York jazz was still regarded by many members of polite society as the creation of reprobates intent on destroying the very fabric of civilization. Also, jazz musicians in this period were overwhelmingly black while most of the vitriolic critics of jazz were white. White ministers preached against jazz, saying it debauched young people and corrupted their morals, even their capacity to receive the love of God. White intellectuals charged that jazz appealed to primitive instincts that kept African Americans in virtual slavery by denying them more sophisticated—that is, whiter—tastes in music and literature. White civic leaders linked jazz to the lawlessness that characterized so much of the night life during Prohibition—which many of them enjoyed when they thought they could get away with it. The Jazz Age in its early years attracted vast numbers of critics, even as it drew growing numbers of fans, even from the white community.

Before Armstrong's arrival, New Yorkers attending a performance by Fletcher Henderson's "orchestra," as he called it, heard mostly the popular songs of the day. They were presented as dance music, usually in settings where rough behavior was seldom present. Henderson's group played in some of the best clubs and dance halls in the Harlem section of Manhattan, which was on its way to becoming the capital of African-American arts and literature, developing the cultural outpouring that came to be known as the Harlem Renaissance. Nothing suggests that Henderson was dissatisfied with the work habits or the quality of sound being put out by his musicians. But he looked to add something different to his sound, something a little edgier, and he remembered hearing Armstrong in New Orleans. He had kept up with Armstrong's career through the musicians' grapevine and knew he had been playing with King Oliver in Chicago. He was delighted that Armstrong accepted his invitation to come to New York.

Joining Henderson at this time had special significance for Armstrong, so important was the bandleader's presence in New York. As Laurence Bergreen writes, "By 1923, Henderson had won a reputation as a new style of jazz musician, polished, aloof, even inscrutable." No one knew it at the time, but Henderson was pioneering the sound that soon became the most important force in popular music—swing. Yet he was among those who seemed not to recognize the importance of what he and his orchestra were doing. When people asked him about his developing style, how he came up with his ideas, who influenced him, he simply smiled, offering nothing to satisfy their curiosity. Critics, even those writing for African-American newspapers, said his orchestra was so good it could be compared favorably to white groups. Paul Whiteman, the white bandleader who had done much to make jazz popular and, to an extent, acceptable in the northeastern United States, told some fellow musicians after hearing Henderson's band, "If Fletcher was a white man, he would be a millionaire." Like the comments of black critics, Whiteman's praise was meant as a compliment. People who grasped the potential greatness of Henderson and his orchestra knew they faced limits that white bands did not encounter. Bergreen adds, "The same could be said of many other black entertainers and artists, including Louis Armstrong."

Whiteman had heard Armstrong in Chicago when he and his musicians came to listen to Oliver's band, looking for ideas for their own music. Oliver worried they would steal his tunes, so when they asked him about a particular song he called out whatever made-up title popped into his head. Lil Hardin and the other musicians wondered why all these white musicians kept coming to see them, what they were up to. It seemed that Whiteman and his band were doing more than just trying to pick up ideas they could use in their own playing. Hardin and the others later figured out what a great many other black jazz musicians realized, that Whiteman and his colleagues were in the early stages of trying to domesticate jazz, to make it more palatable to middle-class white audiences by making it sound more refined, less raw. In the meantime, though, they were fascinated by the Creole Jazz Band and its second cornetist. In New York, Whiteman realized that Henderson had the potential to make that same sound. But he knew what Henderson apparently did not know—that there were limits to the sound that Henderson could achieve. Henderson's sound was certainly not raw, but with Louis Armstrong in the band it would most definitely not be what anyone could call domesticated. Some tunes they did, such as "I Miss My Swiss," combined fairly tame dance music with a "hot" closing solo. But Armstrong could be counted on to provide much of the band's heat.

None of this mattered to Armstrong. He enjoyed working with Henderson and being in New York, including the opportunity to travel around the Northeast and New England. Almost single-handedly he set about making the instrumental solo a fixture in jazz performance. He also did his first singing on record with Henderson. And he began to make a name for himself outside the circles of his fellow musicians. He had had a small following of fans in Chicago, despite playing in King Oliver's shadow, but his principal fame had been among musicians who recognized in him something special, something they wanted to emulate. There are stories of musicians in Chicago who would ride around in taxis hanging their heads out the window trying to get sore throats so they could sing like Armstrong. But he never became a household name in Chicago. Fletcher Henderson took him off a leash. He often played in the background on Henderson's arrangements of songs the band performed in live appearances, but increasingly Henderson called on him to play solos, especially in recordings they made together.

Those recordings electrified not only the jazz subculture in New York but the general population of music lovers. Armstrong was not simply reciting the duet figures he and

Oliver had worked out on their recordings, as exciting and pathbreaking as those were. The improvising he began doing with Henderson consisted of solos that elaborated the melodies and harmonies in Henderson's arrangements. Armstrong did not stray far from the outlines provided by the written arrangements. But his sense of the blues showed up in much of his work with Henderson's band, which largely lacked an acquaintance with the blues, and provided him with an emotional range that he used to set his music apart, dramatically, from what everyone else was playing. This can be heard especially in Armstrong's playing in "Sugarfoot Stomp," in which his solos feature frequent use of "blue" notes, the flattened third, fifth, or seventh notes in a scale, a common practice of blues performers attempting to increase the emotional tension in a piece of music. Armstrong was able to demonstrate how rewarding it could be when a musician had the freedom to step out from what was written by someone else, often someone who did not even appear on stage playing the songs he had arranged. Armstrong did not mind playing written arrangements. No serious professional musician of the day would have questioned them. But he showed in his recordings with Henderson that greater creativity lay just beyond the edges of what the arranger had in mind, if only the musician had permission to seek it out.

Armstrong had hit his stride as a professional musician at a time when strange things were happening in the United States. Permissiveness and narrow-mindedness seemed to many people to be vying for the soul of the nation as jazz contributed to the revolutionary feeling in the air. There were plenty of good reasons why many people called it the "Jazz Age." Armstrong embodied the changes, helped bring many of them about, and perhaps more than any other musician, any other public figure, applied the heat that made the period so remarkable.

CHAPTER FOUR

An Independent Musician

જી Despite the relative freedom he experienced with Fletcher Henderson, before long Armstrong began to chafe under the restrictions of Henderson's band. He appreciated Henderson's allowing him to perform solos in live performances and on records. But he always wanted to sing more than he had been able to do in Chicago. He sang a little with Henderson, sometimes with great popularity among live audiences, and sang a few brief lines on one recording they made together. But Henderson never realized how popular Armstrong's singing might be and refused to allow him to sing anywhere near as much as he wanted. This bothered Louis.

In a way, it was odd that Henderson limited him at all. As a bandleader Henderson was frequently lax in the demands he placed on his musicians, who often seemed content to bask in the glory of having well-paying jobs and resting on the laurels they received from being in a prominent musical group. Henderson himself was also remarkably undisciplined. He tolerated laxness in rehearsals, which led to occasional lapses on the bandstand. Armstrong, on the other hand, by his own testimony and that of others, was highly serious as a musician. Many people underestimated his work ethic because of his fun-loving, easygoing manner off the bandstand and because of his exuberant playing style on it. But Armstrong was in deadly earnest about everything having to do with music.

Few casual observers recognized one of Armstrong's most important characteristics that set him apart from other musicians: his absolute devotion to playing accurately when accuracy was called for and decisively when leeway existed. As any horn player discovered who tried to "cut" Armstrong, he could be an absolute tiger on stage. He would slice to ribbons anyone who tried to outplay him or show him up in those cutting sessions, which were akin to the practice some called the "battle of the bands." Quite often, especially in New Orleans but not only there, a musician or a band would get off work and go to hear another band. Old-timers called this practice "sweating out" another band because the group on stage nearly always knew the musicians who had come to hear them and knew they were there not just to enjoy the show. They were there to pick up ideas, to learn new ways to play, and to criticize their rivals, as Paul Whiteman's group had done with the Creole Jazz Band in Chicago.

"Cutting" could be nerve-racking. In New Orleans the technique was tricky because of its battle dimensions. One musician or band would play a number, and the next band would try to outdo it. Plenty was at stake, and reputations were made or broken on the spot. Cutting another band was how some said Joe "King" Oliver got his nickname—though there are other versions of how he got it—and New Orleans musicians often told the story of how the legendary Buddy Bolden had beaten John Robichaux in a cutting contest. In New York clubs, players would ask to sit in with Henderson's band so they could try to cut Armstrong, to bring him down the way gunfighters are said to have approached each other in the Old West, especially as a way to make a name for themselves. But no one seems to have succeeded in cutting Louis.

People generally neglected two key features of Armstrong's personality. First was that, for all his gregariousness, he was to a great extent a loner. After a show, and after entertaining crowds of fans, friends, and moochers in his dressing room, he would often return to his hotel room and write. He always carried a typewriter with him on his travels, and he used it to write letters, keeping up with friends. But he also used it to set down his reflections amounting to journal entries. He wrote what amounted to letters to himself.

Second was his serious approach to his music. His solos showed this professionalism. They are not simply played, they are organized. They might be improvised; Armstrong's fast mind and nimble technique could make previously unheard-of things come out of a brass instrument. But they reflected a sense of discipline and a devotion to musicianship that disproved any notion he was just fooling around.

To some it was a great irony that Armstrong grew impatient with the poor work ethic of some of his fellow members of the Fletcher Henderson Orchestra. They had come up in life with vastly greater advantages than he had ever dreamed of, yet they were content to think well of themselves and enjoy the limelight of their privileged position. Armstrong wanted to be somebody, there is no mistaking that. But he came to New York not to strut around and act as if he had made it already. He came to town to work.

After a little more than a year with Henderson, Armstrong was on his way out. During his time in New York he came to be in great demand as a performer and was invited to record with other groups, including the Clarence Williams Blue Five, which featured the famed clarinetist Sidney Bechet, whom Armstrong had followed around as a kid in New Orleans. Here he was, in New York, recording with the great Bechet and creating electrifying music. Some of this recording work came to Armstrong through Henderson, who was frequently invited to supply accompanists for recording sessions. Armstrong also recorded with the legendary blues singer Ma Rainey and Her Georgian Jazz Band and with the "Empress of the Blues," Bessie Smith. But his life was missing several things, including his wife. Lil had moved back to Chicago to care for her ailing mother. Once again she helped convince Armstrong that his future was limited by staying where he was, this time in New York. Despite his confidence as a player, he continued to lack a sense of control over his life and career. In the absence of a professional manager, Armstrong relied on Lil for direction. She persuaded him to return to Chicago in late 1925.

Most knowledgeable jazz observers, even at the time, believed Chicago was a better town than New York for jazz. Armstrong had helped Fletcher Henderson's band loosen up its sound, make it swing more, and the band had advanced the cause of jazz in New York. But it was dominated by musicians who were classically trained. Many of them found it difficult to break out and exploit jazz's fullest potential. The best bands in New York and the most invigorating recordings made there tended to feature a heavy involvement of musicians from New Orleans and other places in the South and the Midwest. Their relatively disadvantaged backgrounds and experiences had proved advantageous to them in helping shape the jazz revolution that seemed beyond the abilities of technically more sophisticated musicians. Armstrong left Henderson on good terms and went to work with a band led by his wife, who had set up shop at the Dreamland Café on Chicago's South Side.

Armstrong was welcomed back to Chicago like a returning hero. He was still appreciated mainly by his fellow musicians and the newspaper and magazine writers who helped fuel the jazz craze that was reaching its peak. But notices in the papers and the chatter of fans who wanted to appear "in the know" generated a great deal of excitement about Armstrong's return to Chicago. He worked in a variety of venues, both dance halls and theaters, such as the job he got with Erskine Tate's Symphony Orchestra. Tate's was a prestigious group that frequently featured the best and most popular musicians in jazz. While Armstrong was with them their principal venue was the Vendome Theater on the South Side, where they provided accompaniment for silent films, which at the time was considered a fairly important assignment. They also played specialty numbers during intermissions between pictures. Although Fletcher Henderson had called his band an "orchestra," Tate's group was closer to meriting the term. It sometimes numbered almost twenty musicians, featured a string section, and incorporated symphonic elements in its movie accompaniments. In their intermission work the musicians played more in the jazz style. With Lil's encouragement, Armstrong joined Tate's group. Perhaps predictably, he became the star of the show, especially dominating the band's performances during intermissions.

As a consequence of his work with Tate, Armstrong began playing the trumpet more frequently. Like most lead players who had come up from the New Orleans street bands, he had long concentrated on the cornet, which players in marching bands usually preferred to the trumpet. The cornet is a slightly smaller instrument that usually sounds mellower than the trumpet, a little less "brassy." Armstrong continued to play both for several years before settling on the trumpet. He recorded with Tate and solidified his reputation as an exuberant soloist and imaginative improviser, further establishing improvisation as one of the hallmarks of jazz and, to a great extent, the American spirit in the twentieth century. He also underwent two other transformations in his life.

He had become infatuated with a young woman named Alpha Smith and found himself growing weary of Lil's insistence that prominence in the music world meant earning large amounts of money. Although Alpha too liked Armstrong's ability to make money, she seemed to be something of a relief to him. Lil was well liked among people in the jazz community, many of whom believed Armstrong owed much of his success to Lil's encouragement. And indeed he did. Lil pushed him hard. He needed to be pushed to fulfill his potential, but he tired of her constant and stern urgings. Although they stayed married for several more years, he felt himself moving away from Lil in many ways, including her views of what it meant to be a bandleader, which he wanted to become himself. But he preferred not to be in a band led by his wife. That came to pass when Lil's job at the Dreamland Café ended.

In November 1925 he was leading his own band, making his first truly revolutionary recordings. Gary Giddins says of the sixty-five songs he recorded for OKeh Records from 1925 to 1928, "Had he stopped recording at the end of 1928, Armstrong would never have become an international celebrity, an ambassador of jazz and goodwill, a media star, a folk hero, and more. But he would still be regarded as the single most creative and innovative force in jazz history." The group that made this remarkable music Armstrong called the Hot Five, and it featured fellow New Orleanians Johnny St. Cyr, Johnny Dodds, and Kid Ory, along with Lil Hardin. The Hot Five, which sometimes numbered seven musicians, recorded under several names, including the Hot Seven, but always recorded as "Louis Armstrong and His Hot Five" or "Louis Armstrong and His Orchestra." He

Louis Armstrong's Hot Five. Armstrong's departure from Joe Oliver's band gave him the opportunity to create recordings that showed his potential for jazz greatness, especially with this group. From left, Johnny St. Cyr, Edward "Kid" Ory, Louis Armstrong, Johnny Dodds, Lil Hardin Armstrong. *(Photograph by Duncan Schiedt)*

was the clear headliner. Like many groups that made records in the 1920s, this one existed for the sole purpose of recording. What they produced showed the full effects of the revolution Armstrong had wrought within the already revolutionary world of jazz—the transition from group-based, highly orchestrated music to solo-based, highly improvisational playing.

Jazz in these records came to resemble ragtime less and less in structure and in length. Ragtime songs featured numerous variations on a basic theme, often accomplished in long—sometimes very long—passages that called on a pianist or an orchestra to adhere to an exact regimen. Ragtime had given rise to a powerful tool used by jazz musicians, syncopation. The technique, emphasizing a beat that is not usually emphasized, had been around for quite a while in European and American music. Cutting notes off earlier or holding them longer than expected, especially in contrast to a regular underlying rhythm, contributed to the revolutionary sense that ragtime created. It captured the attention of many music lovers by capitalizing on syncopation, illustrated particularly in the piano rags of Scott Joplin, which featured rigidly regular left-hand accompaniment to a right-hand part that continually slipped surprising notes into the gaps in the bass part. Many rags, such as Joplin's signature piece, the "Maple Leaf Rag," involved numerous verses that essentially reworked the song's theme, sometimes changing to a new key but charting only limited new ground. Syncopation became popular among jazz musicians because it increased the emphasis and dramatic power of certain notes by placing them between the regular points at which notes were played in a standard time signature.

In Armstrong's Hot Five and other recordings of this period, the songs drew their power by employing the familiar verse-chorus pattern from many of the popular songs of the day, but filling the pattern with high-energy, imaginative bursts unheard in virtually every other example of popular music of the period. The songs also benefited from often being shortened, compared to the old ragtime numbers that sometimes seemed to go on forever. Armstrong also sang on these recordings. He had done enough of it with Fletcher Henderson's band to know he could create a sensation with his singing. He used his gravelly voice, which became one of his best-known attributes as a musician, and for the first time employed "scat" singing, a technique that spawned countless imitators.

Armstrong's scat singing sounded—and sounds—to some observers like goofing around. The use of nonsense syllables in place of actual words led some critics to believe he was simply hiding the fact that he did not know the words of the song, surely evidence of laziness or disrespect for the material and its creators. That was the more charitable criticism. Less tolerant critics went further, saying Armstrong's use of the technique reflected a sort of renunciation of his own race, making fun of the use of nonstandard English. Gary Giddins, in rebuttal, thinks his singing "embodied a joyous, vernacular, and convincing attitude that complemented the spontaneous nature of the new music." In fact, in some of his recordings Armstrong's scat singing amounts to the use of another lead instrument. He blurred the lines between the human voice and the brass instruments that dominated jazz, showing he could innovate and make music people would find enjoyable, surprising, fresh, and memorable.

Here, early in Armstrong's career as a recording artist, views of his ability and of his conduct as a professional collide with limitations others sought to place on him. At a time when many white performers and even some African Americans were still using the tired old technique of blackface to represent black people and their culture, Armstrong cut a new path with scat singing.

All one has to do to set scat singing apart from blackface is to compare the recordings of the Hot Five and the Hot Seven with those of their contemporaries, the Georgia Crackers, led by Emmett Miller, a white native of Georgia. Like the Hot Five, the Georgia Crackers were a group put together solely to make recordings. Later they would have been called a "super group," so remarkable was their lineup of musicians who went on to storied careers: Tommy and Jimmy Dorsey, Gene Krupa, Eddie Lang, and Jack Teagarden. Miller himself is little remembered apart from the work of his remarkable group, but listening to the recordings of the Crackers produces two overriding impressions. First, Miller assembled a great band. Second, his use of stereotypical black dialect and lines from minstrel show routines made much of his role in their recordings a caricature, not just of a proud people but of a worn-out mode of entertainment that was now passing from the scene. The minstrel shows had been popular forums for a variety of entertainment. Not all of it made fun of African Americans, but much of it did.

Minstrelsy to an extent grew out of the tradition of the medicine shows that traveled through American towns and cities in nineteenth-century slavery days. Although these shows were produced largely by Northern whites, their vicious use of demeaning black stereotypes gave audiences, mostly made up of white people, a sense of satisfaction that slavery benefited the nation. Characters in minstrel shows presented African Americans, especially males, as shuffling, grinning simpletons who got into various kinds of embarrassing trouble when they tried to rise "above" themselves. Even in Northern cities where anti-slavery organizations thrived, whites attending minstrel shows drew comfort from the idea that as monstrous as slavery was, it created economic benefits for a superior race by using the labor of an inferior one. Adding insult to injury, many black performers participated in the hideous rituals of minstrelsy, deriving fame and wealth from the suffering of their fellow African Americans. Despite the continued use of minstrel-era dialect by Emmett Miller and others, the form evolved into vaudeville at the turn of the century, drawing less and less on racial themes to entertain the ticket-buying masses.

Vaudeville became the new standard, a largely respectable variety show, the department store of entertainment. A typical evening of vaudeville featured musical numbers by both vocalists and instrumentalists. The vocalists, usually soloists, might be accompanied by a pianist or a pit band, as was true also for instrumentalists who did not have their own bands. The entertainment also featured a great deal of comedy, including skits and routines that evolved into the comic form known as "stand-up." Acts featuring dancers, trained animals, jugglers, sleight-of-hand artists, and others doing tricks of various sorts rounded out the bill for an evening of vaudeville. When silent movies became available, many vaudeville theaters were fitted with projection equipment. In time most of them ended up showing movies primarily, then exclusively. But in the early years of the twentieth century, vaudeville was huge. It helped create a market for the latest music and the most innovative performers and set the stage for African-American musicians who wished to move away from the old minstrel motif.

For a long time, however, an expectation remained that black musicians, like African Americans in any walk of life, must go out of their way to avoid offending whites. Jazz was so revolutionary because its performers refused to bend their creative energies to white expectations. But once that position was staked out, it was difficult for black performers to do anything humorous without recalling the old minstrel images. Armstrong was no minstrel, but his playful style and use of humor in music drove jazz purists crazy and prompted many critics to call him a discredit to his race.

There were white jazz bands, of course, and jazz was popular from the very beginning among white audiences. But for white people, jazz mainly had the effect of liberating them from the old-fashioned music of their parents. For African-American musicians, jazz could be a broader form of social liberation. In fact, jazz became one of the favorite cultural expressions of progressive political activists in the 1920s and beyond. Although many jazz musicians came from the middle class and desired middle-class lifestyles, many would-be political revolutionaries chose to view the music as the raw expression of the yearning—especially black—masses of oppressed America. Romantic radicals either ignored or failed to get to know any jazz musicians well enough to recognize that scarcely any of them would have chosen a lifetime of impoverished political activism over a lucrative career in the exploding commercial entertainment industry.

This was certainly Armstrong's view in his early years. The main liberation he sought was freedom from poverty. He had known oppression; he knew many people who were oppressed. But he also cared about avoiding the charge of being a discredit to African Americans. He chose to go about his life and create his career with his own ideas about achieving success, having a good time, and being true to himself.

What's most important in understanding is that he was an honest performer whose first responsibility was to use his genius toward his own view of art, not to give in to someone else's understanding of what his art should be. Set aside the fact that he later used his fame, influence, and wealth to do good things on behalf of others, including many less fortunate people. His music stood on its own as a tribute to the desire of African Americans for independence from the requirements of white society. The rules, the business methods, the recording companies, the firms that published sheet music, and vast numbers of performance venues throughout the country were controlled by whites. Armstrong and his fellow black jazz pioneers charted a new course. That their techniques sometimes departed from the ways of white performers was not only revolutionary, it was essential.

Also revolutionary about jazz was the fact that Armstrong and many other jazz musicians refused to recognize contemporary social requirements that whites and blacks remain separated. Black musicians often played for all-white audiences in whites-only venues, North and South. But in many of the black clubs in every city where jazz existed, virtually any night, white people could be found enjoying the music, the thrill of doing something their parents would have disapproved of, and the sense of freedom that blacks could appreciate in greater measure.

The first "talking picture" in 1927 featured the famous white entertainer Al Jolson performing in blackface and singing about his dear old "mammy." The irony of the title of Jolson's movie, *The Jazz Singer*, was probably lost on many people at the time. Jazz was busily destroying the racist, separatist attitudes of many Americans. Rather than take offense at Emmett Miller's group and their use of minstrel techniques, Armstrong and many other black musicians sought opportunities to play music with white musicians, especially Eddie Lang and Jack Teagarden, who played with Armstrong off and on for decades. At this point in his career, Armstrong's approach to racism and to the denigration of performance styles was simply to work harder, play better music, and exude more goodwill than anybody, black or white, racist or otherwise.

Armstrong's second stay in Chicago involved a great deal of hard work and extraordinarily long hours. He played at the Vendome for most of the afternoon and early evening hours, then moved to the Sunset Café on the South Side to play with a band led by Carroll Dickerson until well after midnight. The Sunset gave Armstrong the opportunity to play with some of the best musicians in Chicago, including the great piano player Earl Hines, with whom he developed a special bond. The two played together so well that they attracted huge crowds, including vast numbers of white customers and musicians. This helped convince Armstrong and others that the great popularity of jazz among white people was no fluke and was not about to disappear. The Sunset job also provided Louis the freedom to develop further his on-

Louis Armstrong and His Stompers, pictured in 1927 at the Sunset Café in Chicago, a jazz landmark where Armstrong did some of his most important work. Bands like this one were often put together for short-term shows or recording sessions. From left, Joe Walker, Tubby Hall, Louis Armstrong, Honore Dutrey, Al Washington, Earl Hines, Bill Wilson, Boyd Atkins, Willard Hamby, Peter Briggs, Arthur Bassett. *(Photograph by Perry Atlos)*

stage persona, including the joking around that helped make him famous and greatly beloved. He was doing something he had long done, mixing an evening's entertainment with various forms of music and comedy, moving freely between sets of dance music prominently featuring the day's popular songs and sets that appealed more to jazz enthusiasts. Many hard-core jazz lovers also enjoyed dancing, so they often overlooked the parts of Armstrong's performances that, as they saw it, neglected his true calling. In years to come, they were not so forgiving.

At the Sunset Café Armstrong came to know Joe Glaser, who owned the club and who had close ties with organized crime in Chicago. Glaser liked Armstrong from the start, fired Carroll Dickerson for drunkenness, and in early 1927 made Armstrong the leader and Hines the musical director of the Sunset Café band. It was Armstrong's first chance to lead a band at a major live venue. He liked the experience of being in charge, of directing the interplay of musicians on stage in front of an audience of people who expected to get their money's worth and to hear something special. Times were not uniformly good, though, for Armstrong and his musicians. He quit his job at the Vendome a few months after taking over the band at the Sunset. Then the Sunset closed for several weeks because of legal problems and left Armstrong out of work. He found some odd jobs and got on with a band at the Savoy Ballroom led by his old boss Dickerson. He also continued recording, and in the summer of 1928 he made more records with the Hot Five, which actually consisted of six members at that point and featured exceptional piano work by Earl Hines. Altogether their work constituted a remarkable outpouring of creativity. The Hot Five's recordings that summer feature music that represents the highest achievements of a great art form.

One of Armstrong's most famous tunes was "Struttin' with Some Barbecue." In 1951 he told a story, reprinted in *Louis Armstrong, in His Own Words*, of how the song came about. It offers a glimpse of what his life was like with his band mates and a further sense of how he composed his thoughts, using his famous and always-present typewriter:

"This tune was derived and thought of during the days when Zutty Singleton and I were playing at the Savoy Ballroom on the South Side of Chicago. And, after the dance was over every night, Zutty and I would drive out to 48th and State Street. There was an old man there who made some of the most delicious barbccue that anyone would love to smack their chops on (their lips). One order never was enough for Zutty and I. Some nights that man's barbecue was so good, until I almost hurt myself, from eating so much. One night, while Zutty and I were manipulating those 'Chime Bones' (barbecue), a thought came into my head. I said to Zutty—'Say Zoot, as I sit here eating these fine-tasting ribs, it dawned on me that I should write a tune and call it, 'Struttin' with Some Barbecue.' Zutty said, 'Dush, that's a real good idea.' So then and there, 'Struttin' with Some Barbecue' was born.

"That same night at this rib joint, a funny incident happened. I had been carrying a hundred-dollar bill in my pocket for a long, long time. I used to have a nice Creole roll in those days. A Creole roll, as we called it in New Orleans, consists of a small bunch of money wrapped around an empty thread spool. Quite naturally it will look like a big roll of money. And the girls would fall for that jive. So on this night Zutty and I were eating these fine ribs, when I thought about my pocket. Which I only had this hundred-dollar bill wrapped around this spool, that I used to show off with. I said to Zoot—'My Gawd, Zoot—don't you know? We have eaten all of this food and I only have this hundred-dollar bill—and that's all. . . . ' Then I asked Zoot, 'are you stickin?' (meaning) 'Have you any money on you at the moment?????' and Zutty said—'No man.' Then we both agreed to just hand the hundred-dollar bill to 'Dad' (the barbecue man) and if he hasn't that much change, he probably tell you—bring it back later when we get paid off tomorrow. So I handed Dad the hundred-dollar bill, with Zutty and I looking out of the corners of our eyes at Dad. Watching his every move. Huh. Dad took my hundred-dollar bill, went back behind his old raggedy counter, opened an old greasy cigar box, and gave me my change back from my hundred-dollar bill so fast, our heads commenced to swimmin' round and round."

With songs such as "Struttin' with Some Barbecue," and working with musicians like Zutty Singleton, Armstrong sealed his reputation in three short years of musical produc-

tivity as the greatest innovator in the history of jazz. He was
on his way to becoming a nationally known celebrity.

*

Armstrong achieved his financial independence not by being
the "first man" of jazz but by being its most vibrant, expressive, and exuberant artist. To listen to his recordings
from the 1920s is to experience the musical equivalent of
the great voyages of discovery that ushered in the modern
world. His music featured soaring trumpet and cornet solos,
intricate ensemble arrangements and performances, and
playful, totally uninhibited singing. He took a new artistic
form—jazz—and perfected and elaborated it, demonstrating
the fullest extent of its potential popularity. He never forgot
his origins, but he never showed a slavish devotion to tradi-
tionalism or to the demands of critics. He achieved independence as an artist, something countless creative people have
dreamed of over the centuries but few have achieved.

CHAPTER FIVE

Fully Free African American

ᔥ By the early 1930s Armstrong had signaled his independence from the opinions of jazz critics. Despite his burgeoning popularity, he was already suffering bad reviews for his behavior. From the beginning of his prominence, he was scolded for "mugging"—making faces while he played—which "serious" jazz lovers considered undignified. One of his biographers, Laurence Bergreen, attributed this habit to "his addiction to crude clowning." Gary Giddins, on the other hand, thought it was of a piece with the construction of Armstrong's career, that it flowed from his desire to be "true to himself" rather than to critics with rigid views of what jazz was and how people ought to play it. He also believed he could transcend the racist ideas of the time. He denied that jazz was "black" music, though African Americans had pioneered and developed its earliest stages and though they excelled in its composition and performance in numbers vastly greater than their percentage of the American population. He did not wish jazz to be limited in any way, even if that meant "his" people would not get the bulk of the credit for it. He saw the claim that jazz was "black music" as an attempt to control it, limit it, even quarantine it.

Armstrong in fact made a point of performing with white musicians. He did this when he thought a musician could play well and could add something new and unexpected to his own musical horizons, and sometimes the musicians who did that were white. He did not set out to play in mixed-race bands in order to criticize U.S. racial stereotypes and segregation laws. The fact that his behavior drove racists crazy was merely a bonus, a happy coincidence. The fact that it bothered jazz lovers who did not think of themselves as racists, however, frequently puzzled him. Sometimes his behavior cost him more than the high opinions of critics. It cost him work if a club would not hire a mixed-race band, even in a Northern city with more relaxed laws regulating the free association of blacks with whites than people found in Southern cities at the time.

As early as 1928, critics were accusing Armstrong of parting company with jazz. His unconventional 1928 recordings with Earl Hines, especially the duets, certainly marked a change of direction for Armstrong. He played with the same power as before, but his choice of songs often seemed to disappointed fans as too "sweet," not "hot" enough. Other forces were changing things too. Times were getting tough in Chicago after a slate of reform candidates swept into office in the fall of 1928 and began "cleaning up" the city. Having organized crime in charge of many performing venues had its difficulties. A musician could get beaten up or even killed for running afoul of the mob. But with Prohibition still in force, at least officially, having gangsters in charge of everything came in handy. They kept the police at bay and kept musicians working. With reformers who made life difficult for the mob, musicians faced even harder times. Increasingly they found their performing venues closed down or tamed to the point of boredom.

Part of the appeal of jazz had always been its anti-establishment, slightly sinister personality. Middle-class white people had especially enjoyed the thrill of getting away with something that polite society frowned on, such as going

An early publicity photo, circa 1930, displays Armstrong's youthful, almost innocent charm that helped create the appeal he enjoyed throughout his career. Many people mistook his cheerful personality for a lack of seriousness. He was, in fact, one of the most serious musicians of his age.

into a black neighborhood and staying out most of the night drinking illegal booze and dancing to the music of uninhibited black jazz musicians. The white musicians had their iconoclastic moments too, it should be added, and the entire scene depended on the impression it gave of being frowned upon by fussy moralists and high-minded paragons of virtue. Suddenly the moralists and paragons seemed to have the upper had, and Chicago was not as much fun as it had been for most of the 1920s. Then, in the fall of 1929 the stock market crash confirmed what some observers had recognized for some time, that the U.S. economy was poorly equipped to support investment speculation and other ill-conceived business practices. The Great Depression began for many people much earlier, but the symbolic beginning in October 1929, combined with the closing of so many Chicago music venues, forced Armstrong and many other musicians to reconsider their futures.

It would be a mistake to think of Armstrong's departure from Chicago as a retreat from failure. Like many people in the music business, he and his friends were experiencing tough times along with much of the rest of the country in 1929. But by then, and still only in his twenties, Armstrong had already become a famous American and probably the world's best-known musician. To say he was the leading figure in jazz was to state the obvious. But because of the popularity of jazz, he stood atop the entertainment world at a moment when the world desperately needed entertainment. So he brought a great many strengths with him as he left Chicago and headed for New York. Tommy Rockwell, an official with OKeh Records who had recorded some of Armstrong's Hot Five sessions, arranged a solo job for him at the Savoy, one of the best ballrooms in Harlem, with a band led by Luis Russell that included several New Orleans natives and the great trombonist J. C. Higginbotham. Rockwell also suggested doing some OKeh recording sessions with Armstrong in New York.

Rockwell had been one of the first white record company officials to recognize the huge commercial possibilities of African-American music. Despite being devoid of musical ability himself, he had a good sense of what kinds of music, even which particular songs, could be made into hits. He and a banjo player named Eddie Condon decided that Armstrong would break the color line. Thus his recording sessions in New York included his first records with an integrated band, including the white musicians Eddie Lang and Jack Teagarden along with Condon. They played hot jazz numbers but also included some of the pop songs of the day, arranged and performed as jazz tunes.

In having Armstrong record with white musicians, Rockwell was not attempting to make a statement on behalf of desegregation. Virtually all African-American and white musicians who had important reputations in the big cities of the Jazz Age knew one another. They often listened to each other play and sometimes played together in live settings, usually in clubs that catered predominantly to black customers. The black clubs were more lenient about letting in white customers and musicians than white-run clubs were toward African Americans. It was only a matter of time before Armstrong recorded with some of the best white musicians. He had known Lang and Teagarden for years and occasionally played with them in live settings. He agreed to make the recordings without a care about the integrated lineup of musicians. It was a momentous occasion, a portent of a better future. But it passed with scarce acknowledgment by any of the participants, perhaps because they recognized that having black and white musicians record together was the next logical step in the creative sharing and borrowing they had all engaged in for years. For Rockwell the mixed-race recordings had one simple purpose. They were intended to open an even larger white market for music that had its roots in the African-American experience.

Rockwell was a rough-edged man who was accustomed to getting his way. He was hard-nosed enough to hold his own with the mobsters who still exercised great influence over New York nightclubs and dance halls, which Armstrong would need. Rockwell wanted to manage Armstrong's career, and he persuaded Louis to return to New York after an interlude in Chicago. Rockwell was disappointed when Armstrong showed up with Carroll Dickerson's entire

Chicago band, but Louis could not stand to abandon his old band mates and insisted on keeping them. Rockwell agreed to help the Chicago transplants get started, despite his initial displeasure, and soon they were playing at Connie's Inn, a Harlem club that was second in popularity only to the famous Cotton Club. Connie's was owned by a pair of brothers, George and Connie Immerman, who fought off various threats to their existence from the Cotton Club, owned by one of New York City's leading gangsters.

Armstrong also became part of the pit band and then an occasional stage performer in a Broadway show based on the floor show at Connie's. In those days and in many places since, nightclubs presented several different kinds of entertainment. In the same evening a club might offer dancing to the music of a house band, staged performances by that or another band that did not involve dancing, and an elaborate scripted show featuring singers and dancers, often highlighting a solo vocalist. At Connie's, one of the floor shows during Armstrong's time there had been written by the great pianist and organist Fats Waller, who had already gained considerable fame as a composer and arranger. When Waller's show moved to Broadway, Armstrong went with it.

It was called *Hot Chocolates*, and one of its most popular moments was Armstrong's performance of "Ain't Misbehavin'," which became one of Waller's most famous compositions. Armstrong had been involved earlier in a disastrous Broadway experiment cooked up by Tommy Rockwell, a show called *Great Day* that was intended to emulate the recent popularity of Jerome Kern's hugely popular *Show Boat*. *Great Day* fell apart in a series of miscalculations, poor planning, and bad decision-making. But *Hot Chocolates* was a hit, and the notices Armstrong received from "Ain't Misbehavin'" marked a turning point in his development as a professional musician and a celebrity. He won the attention

Louis Armstrong and Orchestra in 1931. Armstrong, third from right in front, enjoyed being a headliner but did not like the pressures of leading a band.

and captured the imaginations of the most important audience in the entertainment world, the people who attended Broadway musicals and the New York critics who wrote about them. The strength of his performance and the magnetism of his personality made him an increasingly marketable star who could go in a variety of directions. Tommy Rockwell was delighted. Acting as Armstrong's manager, he began booking him everywhere.

As he had done so often, Armstrong now found himself holding down two demanding jobs. While doing the Broadway show he continued to play at Connie's, and he thrived on the hard work. His music in the recordings he made at the time was exactly what the critics were saying it was: different. He was maturing as a musician, certainly. He had long since achieved essential mastery of his instrument, and virtually single-handedly he had made the instrumental solo a central building block of jazz performance. But his maturity as an artist coincided with, prompted, and created a new approach to every form of entertainment Armstrong put forward from then until the end of his life. He was now putting himself at the center of every performance. He was not simply interpreting songs; he was using songs to interpret himself. As in "West End Blues," he bends notes, plays with time, gets behind the beat, but still keeps the time signature, seeming to embody a level of relaxation that comes only through the possession of pure power. He holds notes forever and slips in and out of the melody like a phantom. It was truly different.

Some fans and critics did not like it, but vast numbers did. Armstrong also began playing consistently with bigger bands. The "big band" era is often thought of as the thirties and forties, but jazz bands with ten to twenty pieces had been at work for several years by the time Armstrong made his New York recordings in the summer of 1929. Some of those recordings were with smaller bands using the traditional jazz lineup of instruments, even if their choice of material and arrangements was somewhat unorthodox by jazz standards of the 1920s. Armstrong's popularity grew with his versatility. He felt no need to limit himself to jazz or to the traditional venues where jazz was performed. He disgusted many observers with his admiration for the music of Guy Lombardo and His Royal Canadians, a developing big band that jazz lovers thought of as sickly sweet. But Armstrong cared not one bit about such critics. He was busy developing his own image, placing himself at the center of every performance and every recording, becoming more and more of what later analysts would call a "brand."

He had been drifting away from Carroll Dickerson and the other musicians in his band in New York, all of whom,

Armstrong's move to New York gave him the chance to play with well-established larger bands, including Luis Russell's Orchestra, shown here circa 1935. Armstrong is at the microphone.

including Armstrong, lost their jobs at Connie's when *Hot Chocolates* closed at the end of 1929. Rockwell and Armstrong decided to separate from the Dickerson group, set Louis up with the Luis Russell band, and book him as a headlining performer. Armstrong's decision to jettison his old friends might have been a calculated plan to move in a different career direction, unburdened by old loyalties. Or it may have been a reflection of an insecurity he felt around other musicians who approached him in his level of skill. Whatever the reasons, he was moving on.

This approach of placing Armstrong in the center of attention gained momentum when he appeared in California for the first time, in 1930. Because of the film industry's presence in the Los Angeles area, that city was already a major media center and becoming more important to the entertainment industry every day. As he had done in Chicago and New York, Armstrong quickly put his stamp on the place. Tommy Rockwell secured him a job at the Cotton

Club in the Los Angeles suburb of Culver City, near some of the big movie production facilities. He was to be the headliner, but the band was to be led by Leon Elkins. While he was in California, Armstrong appeared with various bands put together for separate appearances. Some were better than others, but the Cotton Club band under Leon Elkins featured some fine musicians. One was Lionel Hampton, a drummer who later achieved fame playing the vibraphone, which he was just beginning to play. No longer feeling the pressure of directing his own band, Armstrong was able to enjoy a sense of freedom and relax a bit after several years of frenzied activity, constant travel, and long stints of playing several jobs at once.

He wasn't idle, though. Armstrong responded to the relative stability he now experienced with a burst of creativity. He appeared regularly on radio programs and in films, both short specialty "subjects" and longer film features. In time he would appear in dozens of films, many of the first rank, becoming the first African American to make regular appearances in mainstream Hollywood productions. He mystified many observers and critics by recording with Jimmie Rodgers, the "father of country music," in Rodgers's "blue yodel" series; but he also dazzled fans and critics with jazz numbers he recorded in Los Angeles. He worried some critics, on the other hand, with some of his vocal numbers, which sounded too much like those of the pop songsters of the day. In a pattern that prevailed for the rest of his life, Armstrong seemed to make many more fans among the general public interested in entertainment than he lost among the hard core of jazz enthusiasts. He realized now that jazz enthusiasts cared about his stature as an artist, but that his standing as an entertainer was what mattered with the ticket-buying and record-buying public.

For the most part, his time in California was a triumph. One incident marred his experience: his arrest in late 1930 for marijuana use. Smoking marijuana had long been a common practice among jazz musicians, as it had been for Armstrong since his days in Chicago. In many cities it was not even illegal, but by the late 1920s and early '30s disapproval of the drug had been growing. It was coming to be seen as something that led unsuspecting users into a world of degradation. Many people in the jazz world interpreted this objection as a direct assault against them. Some musicians believed that anti-marijuana laws had less to do with the drug's mind-altering qualities than with their anti-establishment viewpoints, especially their rejection of segregation laws. It might have made a difference that Armstrong was arrested with a white musician, the drummer Vic Berton. Even in California, racial prejudice caused problems for people who rejected the old social requirements to separate blacks and whites. Many associates of Armstrong's employers believed the arrest was a setup, that Armstrong had been targeted for humiliation by a rival club owner who resented his popularity at the Cotton Club. In any event, well-connected friends got his six-month jail sentence and $1,000 fine suspended, and he stayed on in California until the following spring.

Armstrong's troubles, however, were far from over. His marriage to Lil Hardin was in deep trouble, worse than ever, and it had been rocky for some time. He had continued to see Alpha Smith, had had romantic involvements with other women, and had finally worn out Lil's patience. His manager now was no longer Tommy Rockwell but a questionable character named Johnny Collins, who had strong ties to organized crime and by the spring of 1931 had muscled Rockwell out of the picture. Some said Collins had helped pull the strings to get Armstrong out of jail in Los Angeles, but now he seemed intent on pulling Armstrong into a web of gangsters. Collins took him back to Chicago and booked him into a white club called the Showboat.

After a couple of nights at the Showboat, thugs showed up wielding pistols and threatened to kill Armstrong unless he agreed to come to New York and work for their boss. It has long been believed that Tommy Rockwell had something to do with this event, possibly through a deal with the owner of the Cotton Club in New York, which had strong ties to organized crime. Armstrong had no intention of returning to New York at the moment, despite the attempts of gangsters to frighten him into doing so, and Johnny Collins was not about to have his newfound moneymaker taken away by a bunch of thugs from out of town. Collins was crooked, there seemed to be little doubt of that. He took advantage of Armstrong's lack of interest in the management of his affairs and robbed him regularly of his share of the revenues from his work. But Collins did Armstrong a favor by getting him away from Chicago and the threatening attentions of the New York mob.

Armstrong continued to break new ground. After Collins spirited him out of Chicago, he went on an extended tour of the Midwest and the South. In many places he became the first African American to play in previously all-white venues, including the Roof Garden of the Kentucky Hotel in Louisville on the eve of the Kentucky Derby. The tour also included his first return to New Orleans. He made the most of it, visiting many of his old haunts, including the Waif's Home, where he thrilled the boys by becoming the sponsor of their baseball team.

In those days it was common practice for bands appearing at hotel ballrooms and other large dance venues to make live radio broadcasts. Jazz had been heard on the radio from the earliest days of commercial broadcasts. People who lived far from the big cities where the "hotel bands" appeared, who would never have been able to attend one of these legendary performances, could hear them over the radio. Many radio stations had powerful transmitters that sent their broadcasts over a radius of thousands of miles, especially at night when the dance performances took place. Thus people in small towns and rural areas became aware of the great and not-so-great performers who filled the dance halls and nightclubs of larger cities. In this way, radio was one of the principal forces in creating a national entertainment culture in the United States, and one of the reasons for Armstrong's remarkable popularity was his increasing presence on the radio.

Ordinarily this was a good experience for him, but on his trip south, especially to New Orleans, he was reminded that his success and popularity could not insulate him from the power of racism. He also discovered that the audience for radio consisted primarily of whites, who in most communities were the only people who could afford to buy a radio.

Armstrong was booked into a white club outside New Orleans, the Suburban Gardens, for what was planned to be a three-week engagement. In certain quarters there was much excitement about Armstrong's return to the city. Most people who were fairly open-minded recognized that his fame reflected well on New Orleans and took pride in the fact that, like so many of the great pioneering figures of jazz, Armstrong was a hometown personality.

But not everyone felt that way. The night he opened, when the performance was broadcast on radio, the white announcer could not bring himself to pronounce Armstrong's name, saying he did not have "the heart to announce the nigger on the radio." Armstrong quickly seized the microphone and made the best of a bad situation, introducing himself and going right into his first song. The planned three-week job lasted three months. Collins then took Armstrong and his band to many other cities, including Memphis, where the entire group was arrested when someone reported seeing Collins's wife, who was white and who traveled with Collins and the band, sitting too close to a black man on the bus they were using for their travels.

Collins wanted to get Armstrong back to New York, thinking the situation there might have cooled down enough to try an appearance. It made no sense that the greatest star in the music world should have to avoid its two biggest markets, Chicago and New York. In February 1932, Collins booked Armstrong into one of the theaters owned by the Paramount-Publix chain in New York City. Armstrong had been touring that chain for months, and it seemed a good idea to play the theater in Manhattan. Collins also got him a job at the Lafayette in Harlem. But Armstrong's old business associates were not very pleased that he was playing these venues. His old manager, Tommy Rockwell, and the co-owner of Connie's Inn, Connie Immerman, filed suit against him in New York out of their anger for his not appearing at Connie's as they believed he had agreed to do.

The turmoil surrounding Armstrong's legal status now made it virtually impossible for him to find work in New York, though he was able to appear in two unfortunate and critically savaged films, *Rhapsody in Black and Blue* and a Betty Boop feature-length picture called *I'll Be Glad When You're Dead, You Rascal You*—which was the title of one of Armstrong's most popular songs. Both films used unfortunate racist stereotypes, but, as Collier points out, the fact that Armstrong made the movies at all was a sign of his growing popularity. Still, the lack of regular performing work sent him back to Chicago and to California for several short-term jobs. He then took advantage of the growing interest in jazz in England as an excuse to get out of the country.

In the summer of 1932, Armstrong, Johnny Collins, Collins's wife, and Alpha Smith set sail. In England Armstrong discovered the strong appeal of his music overseas. His trip created an instant sensation there among musicians and jazz fans, who had become aware of the music of Duke Ellington and Fletcher Henderson from visits those performers had made to England, and had become fascinated by Armstrong through his recordings. Arrangements were made to have him appear at the famous London Palladium and to pull together a suitable backup band. It had to be imported largely from Paris, where jazz was also developing a fervent, if small, fan base. Shockingly, because Collins had neglected to make hotel arrangements for the group, Armstrong found out firsthand that racial discrimination was not limited to the United States. Numerous London hotels refused to accommodate the group because some of them were black.

Armstrong's Palladium appearances created apparently equal measures of excited appreciation and disgust. Some fans and critics were amazed by his energy, spirit of abandon, power as an instrumentalist, and zaniness as a vocalist. Others thought he was crude. Some shouted racial epithets. On the whole, however, the shows achieved their purpose. They introduced him to a new audience and demonstrated that his music was marketable outside the United States. They also bestowed upon Armstrong his most enduring nickname. He had many over the years, including especially "Pops." But he frequently referred to himself as "Satchelmouth," which an English writer misheard as "Satchmo" and reported Armstrong's use of the word. The nickname spread quickly and stuck with Louis for the rest of his life. He played a few other jobs in England and Scotland before returning to New York in the fall.

Immediately on his return to the United States, Armstrong appeared at Connie's Inn (partly to get Connie Immerman off his back), played other jobs around town, and made records with the Victor Company. He had long recorded with OKeh, but that company was still using Tommy Rockwell, and Armstrong's appearance at Connie's had not eased the friction between the Armstrong people and Rockwell. He played some in and around Chicago, made some lackluster records, then returned to Europe for an extended tour and a lengthy vacation.

It was a strange time for Armstrong, unsettling in many ways. Legal troubles hounded him, including the continuing rift with Rockwell. He then parted company with Johnny Collins, who sued him for breach of contract. Collins had treated him shabbily, taking vastly greater percentages of Armstrong's earnings than any manager deserved, even a good one—and Collins was certainly not a good manager. He may have been dishonest, but his basic problem was incompetence. Press reports in Britain made quite a fuss over the Armstrong entourage and the star's extravagant pay and lavish tastes. One suggested that he traveled with 130 suits and 48 trunks and that his band earned more than twice as much money in a week as it actually did, a tiny fraction of which went to Armstrong himself. As a matter of fact, the English piano player who led his group earned more money than Armstrong did, just one example of how Armstrong was underpaid. Paul Whiteman and Duke Ellington routinely received two and three times as much for their performances as Armstrong did. They were important musicians and bandleaders, but they were scarcely worth more than he. Collins was possibly the only manager Armstrong could have had who made Tommy Rockwell look good. Collins viewed Armstrong simply as a source of cash and treated him as his employee instead of a client. For some reason

Armstrong tolerated this situation, along with Collins's general mishandling of everything from his living arrangements on the road to the quality of the musicians who accompanied him in recording studios.

Rockwell had bossed Armstrong around and taken more than his share of the money, but he had a good sense of what combinations of performers and songs might work for his star performer. Collins, on the other hand, did an especially terrible job of organizing recording sessions. Virtually everyone agrees the Victor sessions he produced were a disaster. Armstrong got his fill of Collins on their second trip to Europe and fired him. He was also experiencing romantic complications. His divorce settlement from Lil Hardin had cost him a great deal of money, bringing an end to a marriage that had been almost nonexistent for years; meanwhile Alpha Smith was pressing him to marry her.

Armstrong also found himself in a serious medical situation that jeopardized his entire career. He had always played the cornet and trumpet using several unorthodox methods. Like many largely self-taught musicians, especially those who display a dazzling talent at an early age, Armstrong had picked up some bad habits as a player. His early experiences as a musician had been so successful that few people, including himself, thought he needed to correct his technique. The fact that he never learned to form a proper embouchure particularly plagued him, and it was exacerbated by the enormous power of his playing. His upper lip, which gave him trouble for more than thirty years, became alarmingly raw during the second trip to Europe.

During the European tour his lip became infected, prompting a doctor who was treating him to advise him not to play for six months. He ignored this caution, as he had ignored warnings from other doctors and fellow musicians over the years about the damage to his lip. He managed to keep playing after he returned to the United States and pursued a steady regimen of treatments of his lip with salves and balms. Photographs of him as he aged show his mouth deteriorating. Eyewitness accounts of Armstrong's performances from the 1930s on tell of repeated instances when he played until his lip bled—and then continued to play.

This was a time when his playing continued to take something of a backseat to his singing. In the arrangements he and others prepared for his recording sessions, if a number turned out to run long, a chorus of his horn playing might be sacrificed, but never the singing. Many people interpreted this change as a calculated marketing tactic. Growing numbers of fans, especially whites, enjoyed his singing; it made sense for him to do more of it. Other people, especially his less forgiving critics, accused him of "selling out" to commercialism, craving fast money over solid artistic expression. Few people stopped to think that he might have been playing less because blowing into his trumpet hurt his lip so badly.

After he dumped Johnny Collins, Armstrong found himself in terrible financial condition. Fortunately he found a highly competent manager named Jack Hylton, an English bandleader who also handled bookings for other artists. Hylton helped Armstrong in many ways, setting a less rigorous playing schedule and thus creating the possibility that his lip might heal a bit. He also booked Armstrong into some very successful appearances. He was met by huge crowds in England and on the Continent, especially in Scandinavia. He appeared to growing crowds in major European cities and was said to have drawn ten thousand to a single train station in Denmark.

He got into a tiff, however, when Hylton booked a rising star saxophonist, Coleman Hawkins, to play a double bill with him. Armstrong refused to do the show. Many observers believe he was afraid of playing badly and being compared poorly to Hawkins, who had been in the old Fletcher Henderson band with Armstrong and admired the great trumpeter. Armstrong probably had genuine concerns about being able to hold his own with Hawkins, considering the shape his lip was in, and the insecurity that some observers said plagued Armstrong from time to time may have caused him to refuse to play. But the affair won him no fans.

He left England for France, worked with a couple of other managers for a time, and toured with mixed success. On a couple of occasions he acted like an insecure and fading star, and some observers claimed he was losing his musical gifts. Mainly he was suffering unimaginably from his poor lip. Various doctors offered odd solutions, but the only thing that could have saved him was complete rest, a long time-out from playing. He simply could not afford to do that, both financially and personally. He needed the money, and he needed the applause. After a long absence from both the United States and the recording studio, he returned from Europe in 1935.

Something good came about, finally, from an unexpected source. He reconnected with his old boss from the Chicago days at the Sunset Café, Joe Glaser. Once Prohibition ended in 1933, gangster dominance of the entertainment world declined. The nightclubs were driven by music and by booze, and once booze became legal again, the criminal element held less sway. Glaser's old associations with the kinds of people who had terrorized Armstrong became less important, and the two formed a partnership that in many respects saved Armstrong's career and laid the foundation for his success through the rest of his life. When Glaser became his manager in 1935, he set to work creating a better life for

Louis. First, he extricated him from the entanglements with his various former managers. Most important, he bought out—or, perhaps more accurately, paid off—Johnny Collins.

Glaser then set up a system of management that suited Armstrong ideally. The performer was often unsure of himself in business. It was one area of his life that concerned his friends and associates, who thought he was too deferential in his professional relationships, sometimes even meek. Glaser took care of everything from arranging dates and hiring and firing musicians to taking care of the books and paying the taxes. Armstrong allowed Glaser to take a huge percentage of the revenues, possibly as much as 50 percent. Some of his friends, and at least one of his wives, complained. But Armstrong never did, claiming the rough-edged manager earned every dollar he got from the partnership. Indeed, they both became rich as a result of it. At the very least, Glaser was vastly more honest in his dealings with Armstrong than Johnny Collins had been. He was even more thorough in the care he took of the details of managing Armstrong's career than Tommy Rockwell had been, and Rockwell had been pretty thorough. He was as tough as either of them, even feared by many club owners and musicians. But in private Glaser could be kindhearted and gracious, and Armstrong came to trust him completely.

Over time Glaser also earned a solid reputation for treating most African-American musicians with respect at a time when many white promoters, if they were willing to work with black performers at all, viewed them only as ways to make fast money. At first Glaser may have viewed Armstrong in the same way, but he soon realized that he could build a great career for himself by building one for Armstrong. To do that he had to take better care of the great artist than his previous managers had been willing to do. Like other managers, Glaser persisted in treating Armstrong like his employee, something Armstrong gave back to him. He said in *Satchmo*, "Joe Glaser . . . is the nicest boss man I've ever worked for." While it certainly would seem more appropriate for Armstrong to think of Glaser as his employee, instead of the other way around, Armstrong seldom seemed troubled by the way he and Glaser related to each other. In the dedication of his autobiography, Armstrong referred to Glaser as "the best friend that I've ever had."

Despite Armstrong's seeming deference to Joe Glaser, there is no question that he himself had achieved something notable. He was a fully liberated African American. He had been through some positively grim experiences during what many people would have considered the prime of his career, survived some disastrous business arrangements, and still found himself in control of his professional destiny. It did not matter how he and his manager viewed each other. He knew Joe Glaser would take care of him and that Glaser would relieve him of the worries that had plagued him for so long. It was liberating, in every sense of the word.

CHAPTER SIX

Looking to a New Future

🎵 Joe Glaser went to work, exploiting the opportunity Armstrong represented to make them both very rich. In the fall of 1935 he got Armstrong a series of jobs in New York City, including one in a new club on the former site of Connie's Inn, now shut down. Glaser also negotiated a contract with Decca Records that produced a string of important songs. For years, in keeping with the trend in popular music, the bands Armstrong worked with had been growing larger. They often featured a half-dozen brass pieces, almost as many reed instruments, and the usual rhythm section of drums, bass, and piano, sometimes supplemented with a guitar. As unimpressive as his Victor recordings had been, the work that came out of the Decca sessions showed Armstrong back in good form. He had made the transition from small groups to big bands, though there were important differences between Armstrong's approach to the big-band phenomenon and that of others who fronted the groups.

Indeed, the music of the "swing" bands was evolving. It had started as dance music, which jazz had been in its early days, but in many ways was becoming more sedate. Swing bands played for dancing, to be sure, but they also could put on a stage show in a theater that resembled a concert more than the old variety show formats that Armstrong and his colleagues had offered. Many people trace the beginnings of swing to the work of the white clarinetist and bandleader Benny Goodman in 1934, whose "hot" playing had been interesting but not especially popular. He then hit upon a more refined style that was less exuberant than its jazz predecessors, more relaxed, and more contained. It became increasingly popular, especially among audiences of young people, who are always looking for something to set themselves apart from their parents. At this time they found it in the new, elegant music that made the jazz their parents had enjoyed sound as hopelessly old-fashioned as the ragtime that jazz had eclipsed.

Other bandleaders followed Goodman's example, including several African Americans who had foreshadowed swing music in the twenties and early thirties. By 1938 swing had come to dominate the music world, sweeping its parent, jazz, into the corners of American popular culture. Jazz still lived, but casual fans of music thought of it as obsolete, for the most part, overtaken by the new big-band music. Swing concerts featured frequent solos by the bandleader, nearly always a skilled instrumentalist. But they also included solos by other band members, many of whom—such as saxophonist and vocalist Tex Beneke of Glenn Miller's band, and vibraphonist Lionel Hampton of the Benny Goodman band—become nationally famous because of the exposure they received in these shows. The swing bands also featured tightly orchestrated ensemble playing, with dense harmonies, especially by the reed instruments, which fascinated fans with their devilish intricacy.

Armstrong, who later came into conflict with Goodman, had been one of the black musicians who prefigured the rise of swing. But swing seemed somehow to push Armstrong to the musical sidelines, which was odd because he had been one of the first musicians to adopt the style that came to be regarded as swing. That quality can be heard in his solo work with Fletcher Henderson and in his earlier playing with King Oliver. Yet while he used the word "swing" in the mid-1920s and called it out to his band in a 1931 recording, Armstrong never quite fit the mold of the swing bands. His big bands used elements of the same musical formula as other swing bands, but there were several differences.

For one thing, he was always the star. Other band members would take occasional solos in live performances, but only long enough to give Armstrong a break. They seldom played enough solos to create or enhance a career beyond a "sideman," a supporting musician whose principal task was to back up Armstrong to his greatest advantage. Also, he crafted and used performances differently from other leaders of big bands. Swing bands played dance music, and their natural habitat was the ballroom. But they often played stage shows in theaters, where Armstrong felt quite at home. The style of his show worked best in that setting, a throwback to the old days of the vaudeville headliner. He, not the musicians in his band, was the reason people went to one of his shows. For people who liked Armstrong, and there were plenty of them, that was enough. For people who liked swing music, he seemed not nearly as interesting as the bands of Glenn Miller, Harry James, and Tommy and Jimmy Dorsey.

None of this mattered to Armstrong. In 1936 he appeared in *Pennies from Heaven*, a major Hollywood motion picture with Bing Crosby, one of the biggest stars of the age. Being in *Pennies* was a major career boost for Louis and showed what he could bring to a film project. He added a great deal of fun to any movie he appeared in, and eventually he was in plenty of them, partly because he was a popular entertainer and partly because he was not viewed as a threat by the white movie executives or by the people who bought the tickets that kept them in business. In those days, black characters in movies that came from the mainline white-run studios werc almost always docile servants or foolish, superstitious simpletons. The white-run studios would not book certain films into theaters in Southern cities if the movies featured strong, competent black characters.

It was not only white prejudice, however, that supported this policy. Being nonthreatening to whites won Armstrong a great deal of admiration from fellow blacks who believed that no one would be served by riling up the powerful white majority. It also, however, provoked criticism from militant African Americans and white activists who viewed the maltreatment of blacks as one of the most powerful failings of the American capitalist system. Speaking out against that system and refusing to go along with its rules and restrictions on African Americans were valued much more highly by militant blacks and radical whites than were the long-term possibilities for economic change that might result from developing a black middle class. Armstrong was clearly middle class. He wanted to make a decent living for himself and, at this point in his life, not rock the racial-justice boat. He appeared in the white-made movies, made his funny faces, clowned and danced around, was called "Uncle Tom" by his critics, and drew growing paychecks.

In 1937 he became the first African American to headline a national radio show. For several months he took over for pop crooner and bandleader Rudy Vallee as substitute host of an NBC variety series sponsored by Fleischmann's Yeast. Movies were big, and so were records. But in those days radio was the pinnacle of media. For one thing it was free, and in the Great Depression free was a big advantage. By then vast numbers of families, even among the rural poor, had radios as their cost had fallen. If they had no radio, they knew someone who did, and countless stories abound about the constant presence of radio in the lives of virtually everyone in the United States in the 1930s. During the

Armstrong playing in a radio studio, circa 1945. Jazz and swing musicians often appeared on radio, broadcasting live to audiences throughout North America. From left, Albert Nicholas, George Brunies, Pops Foster, Bill Davison, Louis Armstrong, Art Hodes, Danny Barker.

day local radio stations often hired musicians to broadcast live from their studios, though many also aired network programs, especially at noon. This was "prime time" in many markets in those days because so many people went home for lunch—if they had jobs—and gathered around the radio while they ate. In the evening the great radio networks fed stations throughout North America an amazing array of programs, from comedy and drama series to game shows and musical variety programs.

Because radio shows, unlike records and movies, depended on advertising for their revenues, the people who ran radio stations and networks and sold on-air advertising were keenly aware of the need for likable personalities on their programs. Armstrong's acceptability to the executives whose soap, appliances, and cosmetics were advertised on radio was crucial evidence that he was truly an important national figure. And he was "safe," that is, nonthreatening to whites.

Thus having his own network radio show confirmed Armstrong's arrival at the top of the entertainment world. This was quite a turnaround from his low point of only a couple of years before. He responded to his renewed success by throwing out virtually any restrictions, from the nature of performance venues to his choice of material. In this respect, being on Decca Records proved to be oddly liberating, for the label's owner, Jack Kapp, was legendary for his ability to connect musicians with unexpected song styles. With Decca, Armstrong recorded both jazz tunes and pop standards, including duets with some of the leading musical artists of the day. But he also recorded hillbilly numbers, Hawaiian songs, religious music, and novelty songs designed as much to amuse listeners with their quirkiness as to amaze other musicians with the dexterity required to play them. Still, this broad spectrum of recordings made hard-core music lovers think of Armstrong as yesterday's phenomenon. He did not seem to be on the cutting edge of jazz or swing or anything. But vast numbers of people who just wanted entertainment liked him. Most of them were looking for momentary distraction from the cares of a world growing stranger and more ominous every day.

In 1938, Armstrong was appearing and touring with a band led by Luis Russell, with whom he had played years before and who shared some of Armstrong's New Orleans background. He achieved a longtime goal when he and the band shared a bill at the Cotton Club with Bill "Bojangles" Robinson, whom Armstrong had admired so greatly since the earliest days of his career. That same year he met Lucille Wilson, a dancer at the Cotton Club. He grew interested in her at almost exactly the time he finally married Alpha Smith, who gave him some fun but plenty of torment.

Armstrong had long had an ambivalent attitude toward marriage. He enjoyed being married, but he disliked restrictions on his freedom, including any that limited him romantically. In a subculture of jazz musicians who traveled constantly and met admirers everywhere they went, including unattached women, Armstrong was probably no better or worse than many of his contemporaries. His turbulent experiments with marriage, however, were about to end. He now arranged to get loose from Alpha as he found a lasting, stable relationship with Lucille.

It took until late 1942, but Lucille and he married, and they stayed married for the rest of Armstrong's life. They settled in a mixed-race neighborhood in Queens, about a half-hour commute from Manhattan in the first house Armstrong ever owned. He never had children of his own, but he and Lucille spent a great deal of time and money treating the neighbor kids and their parents to various kinds of hospitality and generosity. Although he continued to travel continuously, he was now probably more at peace in his personal life than at any time before. The combination of Lucille's graciousness and Armstrong's playfulness made them the favorites of virtually all their neighbors. And it was a good thing Armstrong's home life was so happy, because the music business was becoming tougher. As had happened earlier, Armstrong entered a period of professional upheaval, and again he responded with his own brand of creativity. One of the causes of upheaval was World War II.

War is always disruptive, but World War II was so overwhelming that it wrought havoc on a massive scale, both overseas and at home. Like so many other aspects of life on the American home front, music went through a period of constriction, a time of having to learn to do without. The big-band era had seemed to many to be a permanent fixture on the entertainment stage of the late thirties and early forties, and there were indeed many ardent fans of the big bands well into World War II. But with the war it became increasingly difficult to field a big band. A great many young musicians were drafted into military service. Some musicians joined combat units while others went to work in aircraft manufacturing plants and other war-related jobs. A few traveled around in bands that supported the war effort. That last group included musicians who helped sell war bonds, the government-sponsored investment program to finance military spending, while some toured with military bands whose purpose was to entertain troops and otherwise boost morale.

The rationing of gasoline and many other products made it difficult for people to travel to far-flung venues where they had once enjoyed dancing to the music of the big bands. The bands were like many professional sports teams during the war: everyone believed they should continue playing to help bolster morale, but so much money and raw materials went into the war effort that there seemed to be little left over to field a large, first-rate band of musicians, let alone dozens of them around the country. The big bands, black and white, usually employed lush arrangements in their live performances and on their records, featuring close harmonies and tight shifts from verse to verse and chorus to chorus, requiring virtuoso solos and maintaining an often rigid devotion to playing the music exactly as it had been written. Not just anyone could play that way successfully. The groups Armstrong played with during the war had their share of good musicians, and they made some interesting and important records. But the quality slipped, and that bothered Louis.

This is not to say that he found playing music during World War II a complete loss. Something about the spirit of the people who came to hear him play was a refreshing change from the complaints of those who had continually hounded him for tainting the purity of jazz. He was not playing the fancy places as often, and seldom the big ballrooms and converted vaudeville theaters that had been the scenes of so many of his earlier triumphs, not even as many dance halls and nightclubs. The war had changed the landscape of music on the home front dramatically. Armstrong now found himself playing in high school gyms and university lecture halls and in the assembly areas of military bases. But instead of being disheartened by these new, less sophisticated venues, the experience reinstilled in him a sense of musical freedom. Fans eager for a break from the concerns of the war were less interested in musical types than they were in the pleasure they could get out of a live performance by someone who came to give them a moment of joy. Even when performing on segregated military bases—for the armed forces were still thoroughly segregated—Armstrong felt musically free. He no longer felt he needed to fall in line with the domination of swing, discovering that he could still generate the kind of excitement he had created in his earliest days as a professional musician. He didn't care that the money was off and that he often found it hard to cover the basic costs of making a road trip. None of this mattered much to him. He played feverishly, exuberantly, as he had in the old days. He was happy to be in front of audiences, especially audiences with young people having a good time and forgetting their cares and responsibilities.

Bands that survived the departure of musicians to the war effort had to pay large amounts of money to keep players on the bandstand. The war also had a powerful impact on the popular music of the day. It made some topics off limits, cramping the style of lyricists particularly. It put immense pressure on songwriters for upbeat material that told how much the folks at home looked forward to the return of the troops, and so on—nothing brooding or somber, if possible, and certainly nothing questioning the war effort. Probably the most famous such song was "Don't Sit Under the Apple Tree," whose lyrics went on to say, "with anyone else but me, till I come marching home."

Another serious war-era disruption took the form of a two-year ban on recording forced by a strike called by the American Federation of Musicians. Some unions of industrial and service workers had suspended the use of strikes during the depression because of the general economic suffering and bad publicity they might receive if a labor action further damaged industrial activity. In wartime, strikes seemed unpatriotic. Before the United States was attacked at Pearl Harbor in December 1941, many union officials wanted to press for higher wages, shorter hours, and better working conditions for their members. But with the war they largely resisted the temptation.

For example, the mostly black Brotherhood of Sleeping Car Porters, a strong union, could have disrupted train service throughout the country at a time when railroads were the principal method of transportation for the servicemen and war material. The porters and their leader, A. Philip Randolph, had in fact planned a major march on Washington for early 1941 in protest against federal biases that made it difficult for minority businesses to win government contracts. They also planned to protest continued segregation in the armed forces. The Roosevelt administration attempted to persuade Randolph to postpone the march, in part by issuing an executive order assuring fairness in federal contracts. When a black-led march on Washington finally took place more than twenty years later, in 1963, with Randolph's help, it became famous throughout the world as the setting for Dr. Martin Luther King's "I Have a Dream" speech.

Early in the war, though, the American Federation of Musicians felt less reluctance in calling a strike. In the summer of 1942 the AFM declared a ban on recording. The union was led by James Petrillo, who had tormented Armstrong and other African-American players as head of the Chicago musicians union, often forcing blacks out of work in order to advance the prospects of white musicians, who had their own union. The "Petrillo ban" cut recording fees for thousands of musicians, which the union leader justified by saying he was actually trying to save their jobs. He believed that "canned" music—that is, recorded music—was taking the place of live performances, which the AFM had long protected.

Although musicians received decent fees for making actual recordings, they made nothing from the sales of records. Those profits went to the record companies. Petrillo wanted the companies to pay royalties to the musicians who had created the music that was enriching them, but they refused. So he banned AFM members from making records. Many musicians were not happy about this, as it removed what little income they made from recordings. They had complained for years about not getting royalties. Now they complained about the short-term pain the Petrillo ban was causing them in pursuit of hoped-for gains in the long term.

Joe Glaser found a way around the Petrillo ban. Earlier in the year he had arranged for Armstrong to film four "soundies," early versions of what later came to be called music videos. They were "short subjects" shown in theaters with the cartoons and newsreels that people saw on a movie program. Armstrong's four shorts were all based on hit recordings he had made, including what Laurence Bergreen calls "the notorious ode to a happy-go-lucky shoeshine boy,

'Shine,' which Louis, through some musical sleight of hand, had contrived to turn into an affirmation of black identity."

The Petrillo ban reduced the production of records, and fewer records meant that fewer people were enticed into attending live performances. The leaders and managers of touring bands, and those who played the big hotels and other long-term bookings, often viewed recordings mainly as a way to whet the appetites of music lovers. Most fans owned no more than a handful of recordings of their favorite musicians. Indeed, many fans, even in the 1940s, did not own record players. Most of them were huge and expensive. In many communities consumers could buy a record player only at a furniture store. A person might hear a record at the home of a friend, then want to hear the band in person or at least on the radio, which boosted listenership and in turn increased advertising rates for sponsors.

As the war dragged on and fewer people were able to attend live performances because of gasoline rationing, more music fans relied on records for their entertainment. In 1944 the big record companies finally gave in, agreeing to pay royalties to musicians, who returned to the recording studios at last. Armstrong was one of them.

When the war ended and men returned home, the bands had more personnel to choose from. But two problems awaited the people who wanted to put big bands back on track. As government war-bond subsidies for some of the big bands ended, clubs found it just as hard to afford large groups of musicians as it had been during the war. Too, many people had grown tired of the big bands and were looking for something new. Some of them got what they wanted when an offshoot of jazz began capturing the attention of music lovers throughout the United States and in many other countries.

With the end of the war, a seismic shift occurred in the musical foundations of American popular culture. In many of the same ways that the close of the nineteenth century had seen ragtime sweep away much of the national obsession with sentimental parlor songs, and World War I and its aftermath had given rise to jazz, and the Great Depression and World War II had fueled the dominance of swing, the end of the war brought a great change in the public mood. The swing bands that had dominated the popular music scene for what seemed like a generation now began to disappear. Asserting the artistic independence that had become one of his hallmarks, Armstrong kept his big band together until well into 1947, but there was no question that the big-band era was over.

The new spin-off of jazz was called bebop, sometimes shortened to bop, played with smaller ensembles but hardly a throwback to the days when Armstrong and his fellow New Orleanians pioneered jazz with groups of five or six players. It was a more aggressive, more experimental form of jazz. Armstrong did not think much of bebop and even recorded a parody of it called the "Boppenpoof Song," which made fun of bebop and took off from the pre-World War I "Whiffenpoof Song" that featured the lines "We're poor little lambs who have lost our way, We're little black sheep who have gone astray." Bebop figures certainly did not agree that they had gone astray. Many of them disapproved of Armstrong, especially as they grew increasingly militant about the mistreatment of black Americans.

It did not help matters that many black Americans believed, as they had in World War I, that their loyal service in the war effort would earn them better treatment in American society. They were disappointed when the years after World War II brought no more real change than the "first war" had. Few bebop musicians had what could be recognized as a political philosophy. But some black jazz critics and other public commentators did, and almost all of them had one thing in common: a distrust of whites. In this respect they considered Armstrong impossibly old-fashioned—too cozy with white promoters and more concerned about his popularity and earnings than his creativity in African-American music. This is not to say they had no interest in money. They just preferred to make their money from other African Americans.

Armstrong thought they played music that was different for the sake of being different. They were "great technicians," he said, but added, "Mistakes—that's all bebop is. Man, you gotta be a technician to know when you make them. . . . Them cats play too much—a whole lot of notes, weird notes. . . . That stuff means nothing. You've got to carry the melody."

He didn't feel the same about the rise of another new offshoot of traditional jazz in the late 1940s, rhythm and blues. It worried him more than bebop because it drew many of his fans, especially African Americans, away from his own distinctive brand of music. For the most part, though, he felt a friendly sort of rivalry with musicians who employed the new forms, including the great trumpeter Dizzy Gillespie and Armstrong's former band mate Louis Jordan. Both of them rivaled Armstrong in popularity in certain sections of the music marketplace, but ultimately they failed to achieve the lasting and overarching fame that Louis enjoyed.

*

Armstrong's decision to look to a new future, to begin moving away from jazz orthodoxy at the peak of his earning power in the 1930s might be seen as the fulfillment of the very spirit of jazz. Instead many observers and critics saw it as a betrayal of artistic purity. The irony of being viewed as an apostate by iconoclasts was not lost on Louis. He had simply done what jazz musicians did at every turn in the twentieth century. He created and often improvised a new reality for his music, and this gave him what jazz was supposed to symbolize at its core: freedom. It was characteristic of Armstrong's sense of freedom that he held on to the big-band format for some years after many other leaders had abandoned it. He had enjoyed popular success with his big bands, though not much critical acclaim. Holding on to a format after a new generation of critics had declared it dead was just like him.

Regardless of its decline, the big-band era had been good for Armstrong. He had played the best venues, appeared with the biggest stars, both white and black, and become a household name throughout North America and Europe. By the time the United States entered World War II, he was the most famous musician in the United States and one of the most famous Americans in the world. He was poised to go even farther.

CHAPTER SEVEN

International Icon

꿱 As the 1940s unfolded, Armstrong achieved every benchmark of the promise of American freedom. He bought his first home, in a middle-class neighborhood in Queens in New York City. He became friendly with national and international celebrities in every walk of life and in every type of music: pop musicians, opera singers, folk song impresarios and performers, even country and western stars. But the decade was pivotal for jazz, with new forms drawing fans away from the big bands that had become the staple of jazz performance. Bebop, then rhythm and blues, leading toward what became rock 'n' roll, captured the attention of the youth market that had provided jazz with its cutting-edge impulses and sense of daring. Post–World War II prosperity made possible unprecedented levels of discretionary spending for Americans, including vast numbers of young people. For their entertainment, though, fewer of them chose to spend their money on jazz.

Armstrong's response was twofold. First, he did not abandon jazz, as many critics contended. He scaled back the size of his band and in 1947 made a historic appearance with a six-piece ensemble that kept one foot in the world of early-twentieth-century New Orleans jazz and one foot kicking open a door to a new jazz amalgam of his own invention. Second, he threw out all restrictions on his career and his creativity. His music was fully liberated—he recognized no limitations on his choice of material or his approach to presenting it—and the result was the full growth of his stature as an international figure of goodwill. His fame and high regard spread to places few Americans had even heard of, let alone visited. One hundred thousand people turned out to see him in 1956, for instance, when he arrived for a West African tour.

Oddly enough, though typically for someone who thrived on the unpredictable, Armstrong benefited from a trend that helped bring down the huge popularity of bands: the increasing dominance of the music world by singers. This had been developing throughout the swing era, when most bands felt obliged to "carry" at least one vocalist with them. Frank Sinatra was an enormously popular performer who had become a big star singing with bands led by other people. Armstrong himself had sung for years, but this new emphasis on vocalists was different. Whereas jazz and swing bands had punctuated their shows with vocal solos, postwar performances were increasingly built around the singers.

Something else was happening too. By 1946 the jazz fan base was enjoying a certain rejuvenation because of bebop and a revival of New Orleans jazz called "Dixieland" that had begun several years earlier. Thus the country went through a period of rising interest in the origins of jazz. James Lincoln Collier believes it became "part of the American mythology, . . . alongside the Pilgrims starving at Plymouth and wagon trains circling to defend themselves from Indians." In fact an interest in traditional jazz had been growing for several years. A public fascination with "Americana," even manufactured traditions, seemed to comfort many people who felt overwhelmed by the pace and content of postwar change. Jazz drew a certain reinvigoration from this new interest in

American traditions. Armstrong was well positioned to take advantage of these developments.

For one thing, he was indeed a singer. In 1954 he commented on what singing meant to him. In *Louis Armstrong, in His Own Words*, he tells how Fletcher Henderson and King Oliver had let him sing a bit but not as much as he wanted to. "Not that they weren't for it. It was just the idea that there never was a trumpet player, or, any instrument player at that time—way back in the olden days the instrumentalists just weren't singing, that's all. . . . They not knowing that I had been singing, all of my life. In Churches etc. I had one of the finest All Boys Quartets that ever walked the streets of New Orleans. So you see? Singing was more into my Blood, than the trumpet." His singing, he says, "was nothing to write home about. But. It was Different." Also, he was the key surviving star who had been present virtually from the birth of jazz. When Hollywood decided to cash in on the resurgence of interest in the jazz history, it was obvious that Armstrong would play a major role in any film treatment. The result was *New Orleans*.

It was a wretched movie that depicted jazz as something that had welled up from the bordellos of the city's scarcely civilized black underclass—and was then rescued by deserving white people who had sense enough to know what to do with it. The movie played one important role, however. It portrayed jazz in a positive light and focused especially on Armstrong, providing what Giddins called a "backwater against the new music coming to life after World War II." Armstrong basked in the glow of renewed media attention, which emphasized the link he provided to the origins of jazz rather than his more recent service as the clowning swing bandleader. He was characterized as a jazz genius who had arisen from the slums of New Orleans to take the world by storm. He also basked in the warmth of his own return to the small-band format. By 1947, regardless of other forces at work in the marketplace of culture and ideas, Armstrong was back on track.

Joe Glaser had been after him for years to return to playing with a smaller group, possibly because it was so expensive to maintain a big band. Armstrong had played around with the idea and had even recorded some covers of old Hot Fives tunes. But when he committed to Glaser's idea, whatever the reasons, the change was electrifying. With a small group that resembled, at least in the number of players and instruments, the old groups that had created jazz in New Orleans ensembles, Armstrong did a triumphant show at Carnegie Hall led by a fellow New Orleanian, clarinetist Edmond Hall. And he began appearing with an all-star lineup at Town Hall. He found a new future. It was rooted to a great extent in his own past, in that he began touring with a band made up of five or six pieces. But this departure was loaded with a special kind of meaning because jazz had always been about change.

Jazz had begun life as music for rough times in houses of prostitution and honky-tonks, and at street parades. Moving to concert venues had an unavoidable impact on how the music was played and consumed. It had been music for expressing primal emotions and celebrating uninhibited impulses in settings where anything might happen, including death on a dance floor. Now an audience listened to it while sitting politely in a concert hall. A performance of this sort gave instrumentalists a chance to show off their skill, but it provided them very little encouragement to do what they had done so spectacularly in the old nightclubs—innovate and experiment, take chances, prod one another to outdo what they had done before, to play beyond what they knew. As exciting as all of that had been, and as stifling as many

Armstrong with trombonist Trummy Young and clarinetist Ed Hall. By the 1950s, jazz was long identified in the public mind with concerts rather than with dancing, as it had been in its early years. *(Photograph by Grauman Marks)*

observers regarded the concert format, the new approach seemed to satisfy Armstrong. He enjoyed playing many of the old songs, content to try new arrangements or tempos rather than explore uncharted territory. He would add a popular song to his playlist and feel good enough about staying fresh, but he was not much interested in pushing the edges of jazz.

But in another way Armstrong was deep into forming a new identity for himself. It drew on the past but represented his future, indeed, the rest of his life. He was remaking himself, now the leader of a musical format that was quickly becoming known as the "jazz combo," which would dominate the creation and presentation of jazz music from the late 1940s on. Although the instrumentation and size of the group were reminiscent of the old bands from New Orleans, several things were different. For one, Armstrong's All Stars were truly that. Despite the humbling realization that most of them were available only because they were without jobs or had lost bands they had been leading in the sudden decline of the big bands, they were stars. The personnel varied from job to job but often included Jack Teagarden, Trummy Young, Tyree Glenn, Barney Bigard, Earl Hines, Cozy Cole, Milt Hinton, and others in the very top ranks of jazz. It was certainly the highest-paid small jazz group working anywhere.

Many jazz lovers were elated. *Time* magazine ran a column praising Armstrong for shunning commercialism and returning to jazz—though Joe Glaser was now asking, and getting, $4,000 a week for the group, a huge sum at the time. As long as they were willing to endure the rigors of constant travel, the band was assured seemingly endless work. Armstrong liked one-night stands. He enjoyed the kick of lighting up a different group of people every night, which grew in part out of his sense of egalitarianism. He knew he could make a perfectly nice living playing in New York, and, after all, that was where he owned a home. He could have gone to work and slept in his own bed much more often than he did. But he said in 1957 that he went to the smaller places around the country because those people usually did not have a chance to hear him, and he wanted people to hear him. His sense of fairness also applied to the band. On many of his tours, when he had plenty of money and could have traveled in great style, he usually insisted on riding the bus with the members of the band, even when he was provided a limousine for his own use and even when Joe Glaser gave him fits about his generous gestures of solidarity with his fellow musicians. On many occasions he let some of the band members ride in the limousine so they could get some sleep, which was often hard to do on the extremely uncomfortable buses that most musical groups used for their long-distance travel.

Others in the band were not as happy to be on the road, but those who stuck with Armstrong or filled in as different members phased out of the band stayed busy, as Armstrong did essentially until the end of his life. His band mates also received a great deal of attention by playing with Armstrong. Of course, he was clearly the star, and that caused a rift between him and his longtime friend Earl Hines. The great pianist left the band when Joe Glaser refused to give him near-equal billing with Armstrong, who was glad to be rid of Hines's ego. But Armstrong was happy to boost the name recognition and careers of others. They were known as Armstrong's "sidemen," but they got the attention and often the adoration of huge audiences around the world.

Joe Glaser deserves much of the credit for maintaining stability in Armstrong's band. The manager was careful about musicians, especially avoiding players with drug problems. He required candidates for membership in the band to undergo physical examinations. He also tried to make sure the band was racially mixed. This is not to suggest that Glaser was particularly high-minded about race. He might have despised segregation, but there is no doubt that his love of a successful night's entertainment was stronger than his hatred of any sort of injustice. He knew that some white people would feel more comfortable buying a ticket for a show if they knew they would see at least a few white performers on stage. The kinds of people who came to a Louis Armstrong show were unlikely to be bigots, but it never hurt to be too careful. Glaser thought some fans could use a little reassurance that there were white musicians who could keep up with Armstrong. His concern foreshadowed those later expressed by the management of sports teams when their rosters became increasingly dominated by African Americans with superior talent and determination to succeed than that possessed by some of their white counterparts.

Despite Armstrong's success, some misgivings still rankled him. It was always a source of sadness and some anger for him that he could not perform in New Orleans because of city regulations and a state law prohibiting integrated bands from appearing in public. New Orleans certainly had no monopoly on such misguided thinking. But it represented a special irony and a profound loss of potential that the birthplace of jazz, a place steeped in personal freedom, could not accept one of the basic extensions of freedom that jazz had helped bring about. Armstrong had slipped into New Orleans once, in 1949, but remained largely in a state of self-exile from the city of his birth.

That 1949 visit was to preside as King of the Zulus. The Zulu Social Aid and Pleasure Club is one of the groups that parade during Carnival, the period of celebration leading up to Mardi Gras, the day before the beginning of the period of self-examination and penitence known to many Christians as Lent. Zulu is also an African-American Carnival krewe, famous for the outrageous behavior of its members during their much-anticipated Mardi Gras parade. The king rides on a float, and Armstrong was deeply honored to be part of a celebrated tradition that connected the rebellious spirit of his own people in the face of the city's racial restrictions, particularly the ways Zulu made fun of the high-society pretensions of the white krewes, which were made up of many of the same people who kept Jim Crow laws in place.

Of course, critics and snobbish reporters produced accounts of his behavior with Zulu that described it as the fulfillment of prophecy. So much public clowning in one day, while wearing an outrageous outfit and blackface makeup, confirmed their low opinions of Armstrong as someone who wasn't a serious musician. But he used the trip to criticize racial discrimination, which was serious enough. His own description of the experience, from a letter he wrote in 1953, reprinted in *Louis Armstrong, in His Own Words*, offers clues to his interpretation of what being King of the Zulus meant: "The Club . . . for generations consist[ed] of the fellows in my neighborhood. The members were—coal cart drivers, bar tenders—waiters, Hustlers, etc., people of all walks of life. Nobody had very much. But they loved each other. And put their best foot forward as to making a real fine thing of the Zulu Aid and Social Club. It's been my life long ambition to become King of the Zulus, someday. And the Lord certainly did answer my prayer. Just think. New Orleans has been having [Mardi Gras] for generations. . . . I watched a many white Kings Launch in the Mississippi River. At the foot of Canal Street. He'd get off of his big fine boat looking like a million (which most of them have). The King would then get up on his float which was waiting for him to come from somewhere up the river. Then the parade was on."

Armstrong had watched this action as a kid. Now he was in the middle of it—at least the black part of it. Joe Glaser missed the point entirely, viewing the opportunity to appear in New Orleans as just another job. He even tried to get Zulu to advance Armstrong an exorbitant fee to ride as their king. But Armstrong simply meant to enjoy the honor, and eventually the two sides worked out an arrangement. The appearance was so noteworthy that *Time* magazine ran a cover story on Armstrong's trip to New Orleans as the Zulu king, making him the first jazz musician to get a cover story in the celebrated newsweekly. Armstrong was received by the mayor of New Orleans, who joked with him and had his picture taken. White and black New Orleanians had long practice in knowing how to relate to each other, and the visit was cordial. But no one who looked upon the scene had any illusions that it signaled a change in the city's race relations.

Like countless other African Americans in New Orleans, Armstrong as a kid had watched the dress-up antics of the grand white "fathers" of the city in the days leading up to Mardi Gras, culminating in the crowning of Rex, the King of Carnival, who was always a prominent white businessman or civic leader. These were the people who owned things, who made the decisions that affected the lives of others, who lived in the houses that the black maids cleaned, and who looked down on the black men who tried to navigate their way through life in a city that often provided them a hostile environment. Zulu had its own traditions, richly developed over decades, but part of its function was to make fun of the white carnival traditions. The discrimination that still pervaded New Orleans goaded Armstrong and set the stage for his more extensive outbursts a few years later. In 1949, though, it must have driven Armstrong crazy to think that his music, the music of people like him, had done so much to make New Orleans world famous, yet the city made it difficult for him to appear with his own band be-cause it would have offended people who could not bear to look up at a stage and see black and white musicians work-ing together as equals.

It was fine to see a black band. Whites in the South had a long tradition of enjoying the music of the happy "darkies," going back to the days of slavery. In those days it pleased plantation owners to think of themselves as benevolent semi-deities because they had rescued the poor savages from the depredations of life in "darkest" Africa, brought them to the New World, taught them English and just enough "civilized" religion to keep them docile in the hope of a better life after death, and kept them fed and clothed and always with plenty of fresh air and good, hard work to keep them honest. The fine white leaders of New Orleans were reluctant to allow white musicians, especially those in a band led by a black man, to disgrace the stage of any venue in the city. He managed to play there a few times, and played a date with Jack Teagarden and the band during Carnival in 1949; but he largely avoided the city for the remainder of his life.

Some observers were not thrilled that Armstrong had formed the All Stars, believing that the band seemed mainly to be a showcase for Armstrong. But the group's importance lay with the fact that its music defied categorization. Other groups in the post-big-band era were experimenting with new bop forms or doing the watered-down version of old-time New Orleans jazz called Dixieland. In any event, they were playing music it was pretty hard to call anything but jazz. Armstrong's group was not trying to recreate the old New Orleans sound. It charted a new course. It played hot solos, but it could swing when it wanted to. It did comic novelty numbers, but it also played straight-up, driving jazz that left audiences breathless, all this with a sense of repertoire that knew no boundaries. James Lincoln Collier was one of those less than ecstatic, saying, "It is difficult to know exactly what audiences found so attractive about the All Stars." But Collier essentially answered his own question. Armstrong and the All Stars did not do much for jazz purists, but they provided solid entertainment for people who liked a good show.

This was reflected in Armstrong's insistence on taking Velma Middleton with him on many of the All Stars' appearances. Middleton was a large, overweight woman who sang not particularly well; but she pleased Armstrong because of her comic abilities. He and she would sing duets, often with back-and-forth references to risqué themes. She danced around and, amazingly, could do the splits, something re-markable enough for anyone middle-aged but especially so for someone as large as Middleton. Armstrong liked her. Au-diences liked her. Jazz critics did not. She stayed in the group because Armstrong cared more about entertaining the people who bought the tickets and being loyal to his friend than he did about the snobbery of people who looked down on Velma Middleton because they thought she was uncouth.

Armstrong, Joe Glaser, and the musicians in the band chose their songs without regard to what jazz purists and other critics thought of their playlists. Although the band often jazzed them up, songs like "Mandy, Make Up Your Mind," "Ramona," and "April in Portugal" sounded a great deal like pop songs, not the hot jazz of legend. Their choices grew out of Armstrong's genuine, and sometimes uncritical, love of music. Throughout his career, as soon as he could af-ford to do so, he traveled with elaborate recording and play-back equipment that he would use to keep up with the latest music. Sometimes he would play a song just for the enjoy-ment of it, or record pieces he liked, often so he could learn the music and teach it to his band mates. He wanted to be able to explore any musical idea he came across. He never knew when he might need it, and his traveling recording studio became a well-known fixture of his professional life.

Even after some of his "stars" were replaced with less expensive players, Armstrong continued to please audiences who just liked him. His warm nature, which had served him well from the very beginnings of his career, proved to be one of the principal reasons for his success in an entertainment landscape that was changing fast. His presence in virtually every entertainment outlet showed the same tendencies. He recorded a variety of popular tunes and became a fixture on developing national television programs. As TV came to

Armstrong, seen in the bandshell in the distance of this 1960 photo, still drew huge crowds at a point in his life and career when many performers would have faded from popularity.

dominate other media, Armstrong's likability, which some of the bop revolutionaries looked down on, served him again and again. He often found himself the "token black" because he was familiar to white audiences, known to be willing to accommodate himself to the starring role of whatever white entertainer was in vogue. He used his international stardom to lend credence to the attempts of other entertainers to scale the heights he occupied. The fact that few of them ever did was irrelevant to him. He knew that black entertainers were unlikely to get television shows of their own for quite some time.

It was important for him to present himself in whatever forum he could. He would not be pushed around; he chose his battles carefully, controlling the parts of his professional life that mattered to him and letting others go. He had traveled from a period of eclipse to one of immense stardom. He had reached a level of fame that guaranteed him a place in the news outlets and a large crowd no matter where or why he appeared. In some ways it had ceased to matter that Armstrong was a musician. He was not someone who was, as they say, famous for being famous. He had earned his fame. But it had become a phenomenon in and of itself. To many people who were fans of Louis Armstrong, it did not much matter what his specialty was. They liked what he did on TV or on the radio or in person or on record or in films. They liked what he said in interviews. He was funny and open and often just outrageous enough to tickle people without offending them, even in interviews, which of course pleased journalists and their editors as well as their readers. As the newspaper people said, he was "good copy."

In the years after World War II he was on his way to becoming what could only be described as an international "phenomenon." He had long since grown accustomed to enormous popularity, even adoration. But Joe Glaser had something different in mind for Armstrong. There is no direct evidence accounting for what prompted Glaser to come up with the idea, but he conceived of Armstrong as a worldwide goodwill ambassador. This stance became particularly important in the 1950s as the civil rights struggle began to heat up at home and the cold war began to dominate how Americans viewed the rest of the world and sought to present the country to others. It was also a time when some of the most basic beliefs of the national self-understanding were being tested. If all people were created equal, how could laws denying the basic rights of some minorities be allowed to stay on the books? The country's failures to live up to its promise of the full benefits of citizenship for everyone suddenly became a source of international embarrassment.

The United States and its mostly democratic Western allies were locked in a struggle with the Soviet Union and its Communist allies and satellite states, which many Americans called "puppet" regimes. Many analysts described this geopolitical situation as a struggle between the "first world" and the "second world." Much of the energy and resources expended during the cold war was pointed toward winning the allegiance of countries that had not aligned with either of the superpowers, especially the nations of Latin America, Asia, and Africa, the so-called third world. The persistence of segregation in the United States, and the rise of a protest movement that challenged this unfair situation, became propaganda tools for the Communist cause. Third-world peoples in Latin America, Asia, and Africa were overwhelmingly people of color who would be ethnic minorities in the United States. It was obvious to any fair-minded observer, the Communists said, that America failed to live up to the promises of its own national rhetoric when it came to the rights of its nonwhite population.

Glaser saw Armstrong as useful in overcoming that problem. It should be pointed out that Glaser was not simply a high-minded patriot. He was chiefly interested in making money for himself and for Armstrong. But he recognized the potential good Armstrong could do for his nation and his bank account, especially in Africa. By the mid-1950s the strategy was working quite well. Armstrong drew thousands of adoring fans wherever he appeared, and tens of thousands when he appeared in Africa. Joe Glaser was careful to link these goodwill tours to paid appearances so as not to give away Armstrong's valuable time. The tours were so successful that in 1955 the famed television news broadcaster

Edward R. Murrow of CBS News began filming segments of them for American television. The hour-long program aired in 1957 and was called "Salute to Satch," later expanded as a film titled *Satchmo the Great.*

One especially significant trip occurred in 1956 when a CBS News crew accompanied Armstrong and the All Stars to Ghana. He had drawn huge crowds and rave reviews for appearances in Africa before, but when he came to Ghana he accounted for a particularly warm welcome by saying, "After all, my ancestors came from here and I still have African blood in me." Armstrong felt a special kinship with the people of Ghana, in part because he saw a physical resemblance between them and himself. This was true both in the body types and facial structure of many of the people he met and in some of their behavior, particularly the ways they used facial expressions to communicate, as he so often did. Like other peoples in Africa, the Ghanaians responded enthusiastically to his visit and made him feel at home. But something about Ghana made him feel as if he really had come home. Many African Americans had ancestors who had come from this part of Africa, and perhaps it was true that Armstrong was among blood relatives in Ghana. But at the very least, this was a place where, as Laurence Bergreen writes, "It was exhilarating to be a black man in a black land, not part of the minority for once, but a member of the overwhelming majority."

Crowds that turned out to greet the famous performer were estimated at more than 100,000, far greater than any audience he had ever seen in the United States, where he had a great fan base but had come to be taken somewhat for granted by loyal but modest-sized audiences. Africans were drawn to Armstrong's music and to his personality, but they were especially fascinated to see this most famous person of African descent, very possibly anywhere in the world at the time. Africa was in the midst of numerous and growing independence movements seeking to throw off the European imperialism of the early twentieth century, and spirits ran high in almost any public gathering. Police officials cautioned Armstrong not to play music that was too "hot" for fear the crowds would be whipped into a frenzy and begin to riot. He tried to conform to their wishes, though a performance of dozens of tribal drummers threatened to get out of hand when he was so moved by the incredible power of their music that he began playing with them a feverish version of "Stomping at the Savoy."

Ghana was led by the iconic African liberation leader Kwame Nkrumah, who had studied in the United States as a young man and had become a jazz fan and a promoter of jazz on the African continent. When Armstrong performed for Nkrumah, he hit a special note of poignancy with his performance of "What Did I Do to Be So Black and Blue?" "Transfixing the audience with this musical commiseration and celebration of their blackness, Louis sang with unequaled intensity before the man who was in the throes of creating an independent African nation," Laurence Bergreen writes. Armstrong performed without seeming to be performing. He exuded goodwill without trying to be ingratiating. He won people over without acting like a conqueror. Everywhere he went on this tour, he touched people with his spirit. They responded with admiration and love.

At home he continued to innovate musically by employing the unexpected. In 1955 he had earned a somewhat surprising hit through his recording of "Mack the Knife," which Bergreen calls "a dark, violent nightmare of a song [that] reminded Louis of the thugs he'd known and admired as a child in New Orleans." That Armstrong had sojourned deeply into the land of pop music was illustrated by the fact that his version of the song, which came from Kurt Weill's

Threepenny Opera, remained the most popular until it was brushed aside by the version recorded by the 1950s heart-throb vocalist Bobby Darin.

The next year Louis entered a remarkable, though brief, recording partnership with the consummate jazz vocalist Ella Fitzgerald. Many jazz purists were elated as Armstrong parted company with the popular songs that had become such a mainstay of his performances and recordings and re-turned to the world of jazz. For a tantalizingly brief moment, he was back among the creators, exploring the reaches of melody, tempo, and beat. That he was able to do this along-side Fitzgerald, a truly great jazz musician, brought out the old spirit of improvisational daring. Her own use of scat singing, which Armstrong had done so much to popularize and through which she used her voice to mimic the sound of Armstrong's trumpet, gave him something to play off of that was at once new and comfortingly familiar. Joe Glaser saw these recordings as an opportunity to make money from Armstrong's popularity and versatility. Armstrong went along, enjoying the money, it must be acknowledged, but especially enjoying the opportunity to play new things and keep everybody guessing about what he might do next.

Despite his skills in the recording studio and his trium-phant overseas appearances, not everyone appreciated his commercial successes or the service he provided U.S. foreign relations. Some people who preferred to hang on to the old ways of racial discrimination detested Armstrong because of his vast popularity. They especially disliked seeing him on television laughing and speaking on an equal basis with Frank Sinatra and other mainstream white entertainers. In February 1957, racists threw dynamite at an auditorium in Knoxville, Tennessee, where Armstrong was performing. The auditorium had separate seating sections for blacks and whites, as throughout the South, but opponents of change in Southern race relations objected that the auditorium was being used by people of both races at the same time. Like most performers who wished to stay in business, Armstrong often had to tolerate segregated facilities and performance venues.

But he had his limits, and he hit them later in 1957. That was the year the desegregation of Central High School in Little Rock, Arkansas, took center stage nationally. The landmark Supreme Court decision *Brown* v. *Board of Education* in 1954 had declared unconstitutional the practice of separate schools for black and white children. Some civil rights protests had followed the *Brown* decision, especially the boycott of the segregated city bus system in Montgomery, Alabama, which catapulted Rosa Parks and a young Reverend Martin Luther King, Jr., to national attention. But most cities with segregated school systems in the South and elsewhere had been relatively quiet between 1954 and 1957. Some had desegregated without incident, including a couple of school systems in Arkansas. But white resistance to the idea of giving up their whites-only schools was growing.

When the school board in Little Rock announced a plan to begin desegregating the schools, opposition developed. A crisis arose as the governor of Arkansas, Orval Faubus, mobilized elements of the state's National Guard to prevent nine African-American students from attending classes at Central High, under the guise of preserving public order. It was the first open challenge by a state official to the Supreme Court's order that called for the desegregation of public schools, and it eventually involved President Dwight Eisenhower. He reluctantly federalized Arkansas's National Guard, then sent troops to Little Rock to take control of the situation. Almost overnight, Little Rock, Central High, and Faubus became internationally infamous. Armstrong was touring the United States when he heard of the crisis in Little Rock. He was also preparing to travel to the Soviet Union for a goodwill tour sponsored by the State Department.

He would have been presented on this tour as representative of everything that was good about the United States, from its sense of freedom and equality to its simple love of having a good time, which was considered rare in the Soviet Union. But seeing what was going on in Little Rock convinced Armstrong that he could not in good conscience make the tour, pretending to endorse overseas the ideals that he believed his country had not made good. He was a goodwill ambassador who at the moment had run out of goodwill. Although he had let a great many other civil rights offenses go unchallenged over decades, something about the crisis in Little Rock moved him. He was especially upset by the famous photograph of one of the black students, Elizabeth Eckford, bravely trying to make her way along the sidewalk to the school, alone among a shrieking mob of white protesters.

Armstrong declared the State Department tour canceled, called Eisenhower a coward for taking so long to stand up to Faubus, and said he was tired of the way people in the South were treating African Americans. "I've had a beautiful life over 40 years in music," he said, "but I feel the downtrodden situation the same as any other Negro. My parents and family suffered through all of that old South." He went on to say, "My people . . . just want a square shake. But when I see on television and read about a crowd spitting on and cursing at a little colored girl . . . I think I have a right to get sore and say something about it." He said the government could "go to hell," and that to a great extent black Americans were a people without a country.

It was the greatest degree of anger Armstrong had ever displayed so publicly, and the reaction was intense. At first his friends, his manager, and even his wife denied he had made the remarks. Some accused the reporter who broke the story of inventing the whole thing. But the reporter had submitted Armstrong's quotations to him and gotten him to sign the paper they were printed on in order to verify their accuracy. Even his stunned supporters had to admit the quotes were legitimate. They had trouble believing the fun-loving Armstrong could have snapped so completely, but this did nothing to slow the angry reaction from around the country. Immediate calls arose for boycotts of Armstrong's performances, from both black and white public figures. A white journalist, Jim Bishop, made a special point of attacking Armstrong and calling on people to drive him out of show business. The African-American entertainer Sammy Davis, Jr., said Armstrong, though a "credit to his race," did not speak for black Americans. Armstrong's remarks even drew criticism from Adam Clayton Powell, a popular political figure from Harlem who for decades had represented that part of Manhattan in Congress.

When Eisenhower finally took action, Armstrong was quick to praise him. He sent the president a telegram: "Daddy if and when you decide to take those little Negro children personally into Central High School along with your marvelous troops please take me along. O God it would be such a great pleasure I assure you. . . . May God bless you President. You have a good heart." But he reignited the controversy when he said he would rather play the Soviet Union than Arkansas as long as Faubus held the state's governorship. White jazz great Benny Goodman, who often appeared with integrated groups and deserved great credit for helping take down the color line in the music business, made the Soviet tour that Armstrong canceled. No doubt this galled Armstrong. He disliked Goodman anyway because of disagreements that had grown out of a tour they had once made together. At the University of Arkansas in Fayetteville, students voted to cancel an invitation for Armstrong to appear. And he lost a few other dates. He also got roughed up in the press and suffered indignities at the hands of letter writers.

The outburst called into question Armstrong's usefulness as a propaganda instrument in the struggle with the Soviet Union. People who enjoyed imagining Armstrong as the perfect "token Negro" were shocked that he would dare challenge the leadership of a country in which he had succeeded so completely.

But Armstrong stood his ground. For a couple of years after the Little Rock crisis, his name and career were threatened. Radio stations especially shied away from his music. His television appearances and record sales slipped. But he kept playing, kept traveling, appearing in places all around, gradually living down the controversy. In 1959 he got another chance to appear in a film, *The Five Pennies*, with the popular actor and comedian Danny Kaye, who admired Armstrong greatly. For a while he was held back by the State Department because of conservative reaction to his Little Rock comments, but in 1960 they began sending him on tours again, especially to Africa.

To those who knew him it was clear that broader events in the nation were shaping his thinking and his personal response to injustice. From time to time he had complained of shabby treatment in hotels around the country, of slights and inconveniences suffered by his band and himself in an era when open racism was scarcely given a second thought. But he knew the cost of doing business. He had to go where the fans were. After he played a show, he had to sleep someplace. Segregated hotels were often the only option, but his patience with that old, disgraced way of life in his homeland was growing short.

It never stopped irritating him that his mixed-race band could not play his own hometown. The longer he worked, the unhappier he became about the segregation of performance facilities. Although he loved New Orleans and knew better than many people that race relations there were overlaid with a special degree of complexity, he singled out it for criticism. This was partly because of the behavior of the people who controlled law enforcement in the city. Even after the state law preventing mixed-race bands from appearing in public in Louisiana was declared unconstitutional, state and local police and other officials continued to enforce it, especially in New Orleans. Armstrong responded by trying to avoid appearing anywhere in the state of Louisiana. As a result of this self-exile, he spent the rest of his career playing all over the United States and throughout the world, even in countries groaning under the weight of repression, but he seldom played music in his hometown.

The 1950s and early 1960s changed Armstrong's thinking, along with that of countless other African Americans who decided they would no longer tolerate second-class citizenship. He did not take part in protest marches, which earned him the criticism of many black activists, but he contributed money to civil rights organizations, and by the mid-1960s he began insisting that he would not sign a contract to perform at any hotel were he and his band were not allowed to spend the night. He was always proud of the fact that in many respects he had broken the color line, and he viewed those actions as part of his effort to create a better country for his fellow African Americans.

On the other hand, it always puzzled Armstrong that he was criticized from so many different directions. Militant blacks accused him of being an Uncle Tom because he appeared on all-white TV shows but would not march with civil rights protesters in Alabama. He remarked that he knew the furor over his Little Rock comments had died down when some of his African American critics went back to accusing him of "Tomming." But when he spoke out and had shows canceled, such as one at the University of Alabama and one in 1964 in the deeply segregated Republic of South Africa, which based much of its treatment of its black majority on the customs and laws of the Jim Crow South, he drew harsh remarks from less militant African Americans who feared the angry backlash of powerful whites.

In 1961 he told about a striking memory he had of what he called "one of my most inspiring moments," quoted in *Louis Armstrong, in His Own Words.* "It was in 1948," he says. "I was playing a concert date in a Miami auditorium. I walked on stage and there I saw something I thought I'd never see. I saw thousands of people, colored and white on the main floor. Not segregated in one row of whites and another row of Negroes. Just all together—naturally. I thought I was in the wrong state. When you see things like that you know you're going forward." He went on to say that he thought his music could have the effect of working against bigotry: "These same society people may go around the corner and lynch a Negro. But while they're listening to our music, they don't think about trouble. What's more they're watching Negro and white musicians play side by side. And we bring contentment and pleasure. I always say, 'Look at the nice taste we leave. It's bound to mean something. That's what music is for.'" He held that view for the rest of his life.

The Central High controversy and other acts of outspokenness over racial injustice in the United States helped win Armstrong the respect of some of his former critics in the bebop world. As Laurence Bergreen writes, among many visitors to Armstrong's house in Queens was Dizzy Gillespie, Armstrong's "old nemesis." The great Gillespie realized Armstrong "was the hippest cat in jazz; he had never been the Uncle Tom of the boppers' imaginings." Gillespie and others who had formerly criticized Armstrong respected him deeply for the extraordinarily bold stand he had taken when he publicly challenged the President of the United States over his handling of the Little Rock school desegregation crisis in 1957. Furthermore, "Musicians like Diz . . . came to understand how much they owed to Louis's music and his career. Diz would come by, usually with Clark Terry, the trumpet player, and they would say, 'Pops, we came to get our batteries charged.'"

By the 1960s, Armstrong had transformed himself, his music, and his career on several levels. Remarkably, his last big change, the turn to pop, came during the 1950s and 1960s while he was involved in the controversies over his public statements and deeply enmeshed in the time-consuming business of being a celebrity. Armstrong loved the attention, even the inability to go anywhere without being noticed. But he had to endure the constant scrutiny of reporters and gossip columnists, had to answer the same questions in every interview in every town he visited, had to give variations of the same answers to keep himself from sounding, or being, bored with the whole thing.

This was especially true during the incredible success that followed his 1964 recording of "Hello Dolly," the theme song of a popular Broadway show of the same name. The craze caused by the hit song made Armstrong legions of new fans, people who now thought of him as a pop singer who played a little trumpet. It confirmed the low opinions of jazz purists, though, who resented his old-fashioned exuberance as much as they detested his diverse repertoire. Jazz musicians wanted respect and critical acclaim. Most of them acted as if they craved recognition as fine artists rather than financial reward. Many of them saw Armstrong's career path as not just embarrassing but as threatening to their quest for respect. Armstrong was so identified with jazz that they feared his behavior would reflect poorly on them. The role model of a "cool" jazz artist was the great trumpeter Miles Davis, who went so far on occasion as to play with his back to the audience, so determined was he to appear unconcerned with giving them any say in shaping his art. Armstrong was a throwback to another era, fans of Davis and other aloof jazz musicians believed. He had a work ethic devoted to pleasing everyone who bought a ticket, not just the elite, the insiders, and the initiated. Few observers in the jazz world noted that Davis continued to be one of Armstrong's greatest admirers and defenders and a highly successful commercial entertainer. It pleased them merely to think of Davis as Armstrong's superior.

*

The extent to which Armstrong's revolt against jazz orthodoxy was a conscious rejection of the increasing obscurity of jazz is debatable. His departure from the jazz mainstream certainly coincided with developments in the idiom that made his earlier music seem out of place. In a sense, jazz evolved in ways that left him, rather than his leaving it. Further, jazz became more and more complex, even scholarly, appealing to a smaller, more sophisticated, often snobbish audience in the 1950s and thereafter. Armstrong was no musical innocent. He was a powerful instrumentalist and a canny interpreter of complex melodies, harmonies, chord progressions, rhythmic variations, and tonal possibilities. No musician of severe limitations could have been what he was and done what he did. But he departed the strict path of jazz nonetheless and moved largely into the realm of pop. He gained a reputation that made many people think of him simply as a performer of show tunes and sentimental ballads. Those fans outnumbered the adoring jazz lovers of earlier decades, who had revered Armstrong's pathbreaking work as a soloist and ensemble leader and abandoned him with disgust when he moved on to other forms of music and other avenues of performance.

Perhaps more important, Armstrong's extraordinary popularity gave him two kinds of identities. First, he enjoyed global name recognition as an entertainer. People everywhere knew his music and, if they didn't know his real name, knew him by the nickname Satchmo. Second, he had become, even if unintentionally, an inspirational figure to countless people who longed for freedom. In an era when so few celebrities risked their careers to speak out against injustice, Armstrong was willing to do that. Perhaps he knew that his charming personality and ability to generate goodwill would win over all but the most hard-bitten critics of his comments about American race relations. Whatever calculations he might have made, he nonetheless took an extreme risk. At a point when many artists might be slipping into the twilight of obscurity, he had become an international icon.

CHAPTER EIGHT

The Soundtrack of the American Experience

🎵 Armstrong was not one of those musicians who outlived his moment. In the 1960s he continued to create and to stay involved in the latest trends in the entertainment business, continued to appear on popular TV variety shows, continued to be a force in the music of the United States and the world. It was a difficult landscape for a sixty-something musician, especially with the British invasion in full swing. The Beatles and the seemingly endless supply of other bands and soloists from Britain appeared to sweep everything before them, even the American teen idols who had begun to dominate radio air time and record sales. Whether they came from the east or the west side of the Atlantic Ocean, however, the popular musical performers of the day tended to have one thing in common: youth.

It seemed unlikely that Armstrong could compete with this changing tide in musical tastes, especially in jazz. The most innovative jazz musicians, such as Miles Davis and John Coltrane, were making increasingly sophisticated music that Armstrong could not rival. Those musicians were charting the new, creative territory of jazz while Armstrong seemed to many people to be stuck in the past, playing the same, tired old songs, or, worse, mired in a present that obliged him to play new but dull popular songs. He had once been the most vital of jazz musicians, but now he confronted a departure that he neither understood nor cared to join. As Armstrong had prophesied, "jazz was becoming more specialized and losing its audience." This was not just a personal disappointment to Armstrong. It seemed as if the world was passing him by.

The success of "Hello Dolly" reflected Armstrong's drive to keep plugging, no matter the changes of circumstance. For example, he always took advantage of the latest developments in recording technology, including the advent of the long-playing format that allowed him to explore thematic material, such as W. C. Handy and Fats Waller tribute albums. When LPs slumped in the early sixties as 45-rpm records became extraordinarily popular, Armstrong capitalized on that too. As Hugues Panassie writes in his book *Louis Armstrong*, "This is why, in December, 1963, the Kapp Company recorded 'Hello Dolly' and 'A Lot of Livin' to Do' [on the flip side] by Louis and his All Stars with the addition of a banjo [and the later addition of a string section]. 'Hello Dolly' was an immediate success and such a great hit that the sales largely exceeded those of Louis' previous best sellers like 'Blueberry Hill,' 'C'est Si Bon,' and 'Mack the Knife.' . . . The record world was both flabbergasted and bewildered."

It was such an unlikely hit that Armstrong and his band had no idea of the song's success. He was on tour, playing a job in Puerto Rico. Joe Glaser's office staff called to tell him to get the All Stars ready to start playing "Hello Dolly" in live appearances, that they had a hit on their hands. No one in the band, including Armstrong, even remembered the song. No one had the sheet music. They looked all over San Juan for a store that might have it, hoping to get some idea of what the fuss was about. Finally, a copy of the sheet music arrived from Joe Glaser, and they got together and learned the song. They still had a hard time believing there was anything special about it until they played it for the first time before a live audience in San Juan. The crowd went wild, having been sold on the song by constant radio play and by the keen attention that Puerto Ricans paid to popular music on the mainland United States. The band took eight curtain calls. Armstrong was finally convinced he did indeed have a hit.

For the rest of his life and career, pop associations that accompanied his success with "Hello Dolly" dominated the ways people thought of Armstrong and his music. Jazz enthusiasts were scandalized but not surprised by Armstrong's recording of "Hello Dolly." They had long since concluded that he had sold out to popular music, and "Hello Dolly" was proof positive. It was linked to the world of the Broadway musical, anathema to serious musicians of the day. It had a banjo track and a string section, which no self-respecting jazz musician would have tolerated, the critics said. But it was a hit, a hit, Bergreen says, that contained one "striking, improvised passage" with "excellent self-promotion possibilities, for Louis changed a lyric to include his name: 'This is Louis, Dolly.' Not 'Lou-ie,' but 'Lou-*is*,' the way he always pronounced his own name. By drawing himself into the tune, he turned it into a paean to the long-lost persona of Louis Armstrong, who had so much history behind him, and who was still out there singing and blowing."

Armstrong's biggest hit in years was not the end of the road for him or even a marker as to where he was headed next. He continued to work with large orchestras and, as always, with a variety of artists. But as his career began to wind down, it had to be acknowledged that not everything he recorded in almost a half-century of creative effort was spectacular. Hans Westerberg's 1981 discography shows that he recorded more than a thousand different songs, though he did multiple versions of a number of them. He recorded his theme song, "Sleepy Time Down South," ninety-eight times, his New Orleans staple "When the Saints Go Marching In" fifty-eight times, and the pop standard "Mack the Knife" forty-two times. His last recording sessions produced some music many critics considered unfortunate. Gary Giddins says Armstrong's last recording sessions "were supervised by cornballs."

Although he seemed to enjoy himself, even while performing conventional or lackluster material, he was clearly winding down. He had always had an obsession with his health. He was famous for taking daily laxatives and keeping up other health regimens, and being what he called "physic minded." In *Louis Armstrong, in His Own Words* he tells how he acquired these habits from his mother, who "taught me when I was young—no matter how much I drank and ate—when I went home I would take a Big Physic before I even took my clothes off before I went to bed. And the very next morning all hell would break loose in the Toilet before I'd take my shower. . . . All of life I have taken some kind of a physic every night before going to bed. Anything—as long as it makes you trot and cleans me out. I use the word physic—which I was taught to say from my childhood days. Finally I learned to say laxative. All the same. Maybe more expensive than the word physic. They both make you do the same thing."

He was particularly devoted to a product called Swiss Kriss, promoted its use with the fervor of an evangelist to practically everyone he met, and even signed letters with an invocation of the name. If Dwight Eisenhower actually read the congratulatory letter Armstrong sent him after the

Late in his career, Armstrong still exhibited much of the same joy and excitement that had propelled him to stardom almost fifty years earlier. In 1968 he played at the Municipal Auditorium in New Orleans with trombonist Tyree Glenn and clarinetist Barney Bigard. *(Photograph by Percy Bond)*

president decided to send federal troops to Little Rock, he might have been puzzled by the way Armstrong signed the letter: "Am Swiss Krissly Yours, Louis Satchmo Armstrong."

In other ways, though, Armstrong did not take good care of himself. He had a poor diet—high in fat and loaded with salt—in the tradition of habits he grew up with in New Orleans, even after he could afford finer food. He never drank much alcohol, but he smoked cigarettes, a great many of them. When smoking was first found to be harmful to one's health, most of the attention was on the damage it did to the lungs. Not so well known were its effects on the heart. Coupled with his being overweight, Armstrong's smoking caused considerable cardiac stress. He had suffered a heart attack in 1959 while on a tour of Italy and had experienced shortness of breath for years, a special difficulty for anyone who plays a horn but particularly for someone who played with the power Armstrong achieved. He smoked tobacco virtually his entire life and had smoked marijuana regularly since the 1920s—neither of which helped his shortness of breath. He lived essentially in a state of chronic bronchitis, made even worse by the constant presence of smoke in the clubs and other venues where he played. From contemporary photographs of Armstrong and others around him, it's striking how prevalent smoking was in those days. Most everyone smoked, all the time and everywhere. He was no different.

His circulation was poor, thought to be a result of years of traveling in cramped conditions on buses and small airplanes in the days before roomy first-class seats were available for celebrities. He had suffered from ulcers since at least 1947, and his kidneys bothered him too. Few people knew he was diabetic. By 1968 he was experiencing congestive heart failure, the slow decline of the heart's ability to do its work. His lungs would fill with fluid, which in 1969 required him to undergo a tracheotomy to remove the fluid. The procedure would have ended many a performer's career; the young doctor who performed it was painfully aware of the stakes. He could have ended Armstrong's ability to sing, possibly even his ability to blow his horn. The procedure was successful, however, and Armstrong recovered and went on to record again and to appear on television, even if he was not quite his old exuberant self.

Armstrong was shaken by the death of Joe Glaser in 1969. His old manager and friend had suffered a stroke a few weeks after Armstrong left the hospital. He and Glaser had been together for more than thirty years, and Glaser had presided over some of Armstrong's greatest moments. He had never quite freed himself from mob influence and in many ways was still the rough customer he had always been. But he did many good things for Armstrong, who knew it and appreciated it.

Glaser's death was a cold reminder that Armstrong's own time was coming. He enjoyed a seventieth birthday celebration at the Newport Jazz Festival in 1970, reiterating his old story that he had been born in 1900. The event was an all-star tribute to the life of a great performer and human being. He enjoyed a couple of more tribute parties, did one more recording—a narration of "The Night Before Christmas" in February 1971—and suffered another heart attack in March. He remained in intensive care until May, checked himself out of the hospital, and died on July 6.

Armstrong's death was news around the world. His body lay in state in a National Guard armory in New York City. Twenty-five thousand mourners were said to file by, paying their respects. His funeral was attended by many VIPs of the day, including an odd assortment of white celebrities, most of whom had had only a passing acquaintance with the great musician and whose presence annoyed Armstrong's friends. Tributes were expressed in countless newspapers and media broadcasts, including one that appeared in *Izvestia*, the state-run newspaper of the Soviet Union. The "official" funeral in New York was tastefully conducted, even dignified. But Armstrong had wanted a funeral like those he had loved so much as a young man, something raucous and joyous, overflowing with music. That came two days later at a memorial service in New Orleans, with music in the traditional style of the city's jazz funerals. It was led by the Onward Brass Band, one of the groups keeping alive the great tradition Armstrong had loved so well and from which he had learned so much as a young musician. Incredibly, the funeral in New York had been devoid of music, but that certainly could not be said of the celebration in New Orleans. Armstrong had long before come to feel reluctant about performing there, but admiring fellow musicians brought up and nourished in the traditions he helped create played their hearts out in tribute to their great fellow New Orleanian.

People in the jazz community were sorry to see the old pioneer go. But in his final years the pop world had sustained him in ways the jazz community could not. While both mourned his death in 1971, fans who missed him the most probably came from the pop side of his musical family album. They missed his infectious enthusiasm, his uninhibited stage manner, the pure joy he offered anyone who came into his presence to be entertained. They also missed his humanity and his humility. Despite his fame, the worldwide regard he enjoyed, he never sought the company of people just because they were also famous, rich, or powerful. He had refused Howard University's offer of an honorary degree and President Richard Nixon's invitation to perform at the White House. He simply did not need those kudos, no matter how desperately other performers sought them, especially those who had been around as long as Armstrong had. He never became a has been.

That he was seen by fans in the second half of his career not as the jazz genius of simpler times but as a pop idol bothered him not at all. Much of the derision he received was handed down by white critics, and that gave him a fuller identity with many of his fellow blacks who had labored their entire lives knowing that their success depended largely on their willingness to try to live up to white expectations. Armstrong lacked that willingness. Even while performing music that seemed to some of his fellow African Americans as a sellout to the white entertainment establishment, Armstrong was living, working, creating, and enjoying the blessings of his freedom on his own terms. It was a fulfillment of the promise of American citizenship that few of his peers enjoyed.

Armstrong came to be one of the most popular celebrities in the world not only by being a great musician, though he was that, but by being a vibrant, expressive, and exuberant human being. These were the same qualities that marked his musicianship. He made people happy. They wanted to be as happy as he appeared to be, and they showed this reaction to him the world over, on either side of the Iron Curtain. He represented not only the potential of African Americans to achieve an American version of happiness but the promise of freedom America represented to the world. His career had its roots in the Jim Crow South, flourished in a slightly less segregated North, and came to fruition in a United States finally making serious progress toward including African Americans in full citizenship. His personality, spirit, and humanity gave the United States an open, generous, and tolerant image around the world at a time when the principal currency of international relations was force, buttressed by threats, bluster, and paranoia.

Armstrong knew the essential ingredient for success in a society that claimed to celebrate both freedom and hard work: he had to master that society's rules in order to transcend them. He became a consummate musician in a musical form that prized spontaneity, and he gave American music some of its most remarkable moments. As music in all its forms became—even more than film—the most exciting international expression of American culture in the twentieth century, Armstrong crafted much of that music. Moreover he sold it to a world that, though it might have feared and even hated the United States, envied the fun Americans seemed to be having and the energy their music added to that sense of enjoyment.

The famous smile, the ruined lip, the ever-present trumpet are essentials of this publicity photo, circa 1960, as Armstrong entered his final decade.

*

Louis Armstrong was one of the truly transcendent figures of the twentieth century, one of the most remarkable Americans of his age, and one of the most inspirational African Americans in the history of his country. He was, as Leonard Feather says in the *Encyclopedia of Jazz*, "the first vital jazz soloist to attain worldwide influence." But as remarkable as that was, he was much more. Gary Giddins suggests that Armstrong could well be "the single most creative and innovative force in jazz history." This would make him one of the most important figures in the history of American musical culture and therefore in world music because of the centrality of jazz in the twentieth century.

Armstrong gave the country a crucial portion of its national soundtrack during a period when so much of the world's popular culture reflected what was happening in the United States. He could have withheld his participation out of anger or resentment over the treatment of African Americans, but instead he reveled in the opportunity. Even the most entrenched racists in the American power structure had to acknowledge that African Americans had put their stamp on the nation's culture and on how it was viewed around the world. That stamp was rich, colorful, exuberant, and indelible, just like the music of the great man from New Orleans who had done so much to make it possible.

In time the city of his birth found many ways to honor him. It took an area containing Congo Square, where stories were told of black slaves playing drums with Native Americans, and renamed it Louis Armstrong Park. Schools were named after him, which he probably would have found amusing in light of his scant experience with formal education. The city's principal airport was named for him, and his image began to show up in commercials promoting tourism and all manner of cultural offerings. Somehow New Orleans forgot that Louis's triumphs had occurred elsewhere. Perhaps all these honors represented the city's attempts to atone for making it difficult for him to appear there with his mixed-race band.

Although the enduring power of Armstrong's name is tied to his contributions to the world of jazz, he himself believed that he did his most interesting work in the second half of his career. His fame was first established through the music he created in the second and third decades of his life, the 1910s and 1920s. Most critics viewed him as an important pioneer who later diverged from the courses he charted. Yet his own assessment must be considered. If he truly meant what he said—that he thought more highly of the music he created in the 1940s and after—his growth and fulfillment as an artist mattered more to him than maintaining a purity of genre. Jazz critics disliked his forays into other musical realms because they polluted the jazz gene pool, a view that includes at least a large dose of irony in light of the freedom jazz presumably inspired. James Lincoln Collier was among those who viewed his departure from jazz with sadness, particularly the way he came to think of himself and as the public also viewed him, "not as a masterful jazz improviser but as a singer who also played the trumpet. The benefit to Armstrong was . . . immense; but the loss to jazz was incalculable."

While Armstrong was remarkably successful because of his genius as a musician, humility was also a key ingredient. It gave him a sense of what people wanted to hear. He was a kindly, generous, jovial man who struck many people who did not know him well as childlike, because he was not devious or manipulative. Some people thought of him as simple because he could be so single-minded. But there was little about him that was simple except his genius.

This is a word that is overused, often applied to people who are simply good at what they do or particularly bright. But sometimes it is the only word that fits. Armstrong came from such disadvantage and faced so many obstacles, yet he took the barest amount of education and musical training and became a spectacular success. He worked hard, drove himself, put up with wretched living and working conditions for years, and kept moving forward. He also achieved success in large part because he was likable and because people wanted to help him, wanted to be around him, to be warmed by the glow of goodwill that emanated from him. But, finally, Louis Armstrong became an international celebrity in overwhelming measure because of his superlative ability, his genius, as a musician.

Studying his life, one is tempted to ask what he might have become if he had enjoyed the level of training other great musicians received. But Armstrong would not have been Armstrong if he had come up the easy way, with the advantages of instruction and advancement through the ranks of schooled musicians. He rose through the ranks of the street, of the rough-and-tumble world of the honky-tonks, a world where merely showing up for work could get a musician killed. He learned to play on the fly, on the spot, in the musical subculture based on "cutting," in which a reputation could be made or lost in a heartbeat. More was at stake in that world than nicknames and bragging rights, though. Livelihoods could disappear—a musician's ability to feed a family, to stay ahead of the bill collectors, to maintain a semblance of self-esteem. Armstrong had a burning desire to succeed in that environment. He took pleasure in having risen in that rough setting and told stories about it the rest of his life, as some war veterans tell stories of the rigors and triumphs of combat. As some have said, there is nothing quite as exhilarating as having survived the deadly attentions of a determined enemy. If Armstrong had missed that, if some kindly benefactor had spotted him and paid his way to a conservatory, it seems unlikely that anyone would have been moved by his music, transported by his personality, or heartened by his spirit.

No one understood this better than Armstrong himself. Probably he would not have traded the instruction he got at the Colored Waif's Home and the dives and joints of New Orleans for a full scholarship to Juilliard. There is no way, indeed, to know how many African-American children of promise, how many Louis Armstrongs, Miles Davises, or Aretha Franklins lived their lives and died in anonymity, never having an opportunity to offer their remarkable talents to the broader world because they never got a break,

In concert, 1965: the great artist in his familiar setting—the stage, the spotlight, the crowd. *(Photograph by Bob Williams)*

never had the chance Armstrong had. But not all geniuses connect with people the way he did, which again suggests his humility. It is easy to conclude that his humble upbringing gave him an affinity for the experiences and desires of "common" people. But there are plenty of examples of successful people who rose from disadvantage and seldom gave a moment's thought to offering enjoyment to the people they left behind.

Armstrong could not have imagined the kind of surly, brooding, dismissive attitudes and public behavior of many modern musicians. He also kept a balance between his public and private behavior. He was nearly always patient with people who came to see him in his dressing room after a show and expected him to be as exuberant, generous, and kindly as he had been on stage. Even if he longed to get away and enjoy some quiet time, listening to his recordings and typing his letters and journals, he tried hard not to disappoint visitors who wanted to be around the great Satchmo.

He did not spend a great deal of time in the home he and his wife owned in the Corona neighborhood in Queens, but he took to the place and liked the quiet, somewhat solitary life he had there. He never moved out of that house, even though he could have afforded a much fancier home in a more exclusive neighborhood. One opportunity would have put him in a fine house in the Long Island suburbs, close to the home of baseball legend Jackie Robinson. As Laurence Bergreen says, "Louis wouldn't have any of it. 'We're right out here with the rest of the colored folk and the Puerto Ricans and Italians and the Hebrew cats,' he said of life in Corona. 'We don't need to move out in the suburbs to some big mansion with lots of servants and yardmen and things. What for?'" He doted on the neighborhood children, who mostly thought of him as the nice man who liked to listen to music and was gone a lot. Dan Morgenstern made a telling remark about Armstrong when he wrote, "Louis Armstrong had the finest manners of anyone I've known." He had every reason to be impressed with himself, but he conducted himself gently and graciously, a worldwide celebrity with good manners. He never was one to put on airs.

His modesty explains a great deal too about his decision-making as a musician. Armstrong performed some highly sophisticated music, including work with symphonic orchestrations that caught the attention of the great composers and conductors of the age. But if it suited him to do a hokey pop song or a novelty number, he didn't care what those conductors and composers or the cultural critics thought about it. His internal soundtrack had room for many kinds of self-expression. He played, sang, clowned, composed, arranged, danced, recorded, broadcast, and loved in the manner that suited him, mindful of the constant need to be sure that his music gave joy to people.

In this way he achieved the fullest enjoyment of the American dream and the highest historical expression of the long quest for black freedom. And what a lively sense of freedom it was, a freedom that helped create the soundtrack of the American experience.

The Recordings

TO APPRECIATE the power of the Louis Armstrong story, the reader must become a listener. Listening to recordings of his music gives more than an essential illustration of his genius. Hearing his music is the fulfillment of what Armstrong lived his life to do, that is, to share a remarkable exuberance and a high spirit of joyousness through song. Virtually his entire catalog of recorded music is available on many of the common internet music sites, as well as in the record and CD collections of many good-sized libraries. A word of caution: because Armstrong recorded multiple versions—in some cases dozens of versions—of the same song over decades, one needs to be careful to identify the version that was recorded as closely to the time of the events being described in the corresponding chapter of this book.

It is also important to hear music by other writers and performers. For instance, there are recordings of bands conducted by John Philip Sousa. His recording of the "Stars and Stripes Forever" must be the definitive version. Coming from 1909, it conveys an especially powerful sense of what Sousa intended march music to sound like. It also offers the listener an insight into a popular form of music at the time Sousa was at the height of his renown. It was also the time when jazz was rising.

Scott Joplin never recorded, but he cut piano rolls of his music, and recordings of those rolls are available. The rolls were cut by having a pianist play a song on a piano fitted with a special device that punched holes in a long sheet of paper. The resulting piano roll was duplicated and sold to people who could listen to the song on special pianos that could "read" the holes and cause the keys of the piano to sound the notes as if the pianist were playing them. Thus the player-piano version of the "Maple Leaf Rag" is the closest possible rendition of how Joplin thought his music should be played.

An important contrast to Joplin's piano roll of the "Maple Leaf Rag" is Jelly Roll Morton's jazzed-up version of the same song. It was recorded in 1938 for the Library of Congress, part of Morton's attempts to substantiate his claim to have "invented" jazz. That claim was and is unsupportable, but Morton was a remarkable musician. Born Ferdinand Joseph La Menthe, he was one of the Creoles of color who put their essential stamp on the musical heritage of New Orleans and thus of the United States. His romp through the "Maple Leaf Rag" shows in two minutes and forty seconds how jazz took ragtime, threw out the rules Joplin and others insisted on wrapping around it, and made it at once joyous and mischievous. If someone had only six minutes to explain the spirit of the Jazz Age and how it departed from its partial roots in ragtime, probably the best way to do that would be to play Scott Joplin's version of the "Maple Leaf Rag" followed by Jelly Roll Morton's.

It would be a great help to be able to hear some of the early blues songs, but few recordings of early blues artists exist. Pioneering recording efforts were aimed at many other forms of music, because the recording companies were not often in areas where blues were being performed. And they did not think enough of the blues to want to record its practitioners. Good substitutes, however, for really early blues songs are those of the 1920s, especially those by Bessie Smith, the "Empress of the Blues."

Other important recordings of Jazz Era popular music include the sentimental songs of sweet-voiced crooners Gene Austin and Rudy Vallee. Irving Berlin, who composed popular music for decades, was hard at work during the World War I era. His songs "Alexander's Ragtime Band"—not, by the way, a rag at all—"What'll I Do," and "Always" are among many that give a sense of the backdrop against which the jazz revolution developed. The reputation of many popular composers and performers of the 1910s and 1920s, other than a few like Berlin, seldom outlived them; but they were important at the time Louis Armstrong and his contemporaries were turning the music of the United States upside down.

Recordings of swing music are plentiful. Bands led by whites and African Americans alike were recorded. Paul Whiteman's band—one of the earliest and most successful— is a good example of how early swing bands evolved. The famous Dorsey brothers—Tommy and Jimmy—each led bands of note. Glenn Miller was the other hugely popular big-band leader of the thirties and early forties.

Although Armstrong was hard on bebop, listening to what he was railing against is instructive. The same is true of rhythm and blues. Dizzy Gillespie and Louis Jordan are essential.

Listening to Louis Armstrong on record can be done first through his recordings with other bands and then with his own. His first recordings were with Joe Oliver's Creole Jazz Band in 1923. They are particularly important for two reasons. First, they provide an excellent example of early jazz. Second, through these recordings the listener can quickly recognize the difference between Oliver's steady but somewhat unremarkable cornet playing and that of the rapidly developing Armstrong. Of course he subordinated himself to Oliver and stayed dutifully in the background, but this was in the manner of jazz at the time. It was played mostly in ensemble, with few solos and lots of tight arrangements that required each instrument to play throughout most of each song and stay within a well-defined role. Nevertheless it is fascinating to listen to these two players and consider how fully Armstrong appreciated, almost idolized, Oliver. Armstrong's mentor was clearly skilled, but his limitations are also obvious, compared to the range and power his young pupil would show in other recordings soon to come.

Armstrong has solos in several of the Oliver band's numbers—"Chimes Blues," "Riverside Blues," and "Froggie Moore." They are not the soaring improvisational solos of later years, but they sound carefully planned and memorized. Armstrong probably came close to playing these same patterns each time the band performed these numbers. Still, Armstrong was showing something important. In fact, his solo on "Froggie Moore," a tune by Jelly Roll Morton, is widely regarded as one of the most important ever recorded, in part because it demonstrated how much more a fine instrumentalist could do with a solo than had been achieved before. It was significant too because it foreshadowed instrumental techniques later made famous during the swing era. Armstrong held notes and brought them in just a bit before or after a beat, giving them a lilting effect seldom heard in jazz of the time. In other songs he and Oliver performed several sets of duet "breaks," which were a common feature in many early jazz pieces. The band would stop playing, breaking its progress through the song, and allow one or two instruments to play alone. Oliver and Armstrong worked out some breaks, as in "Snake Rag," that became favorites of their fans and much copied by their fellow musicians. "Dippermouth Blues" became a signature piece for Armstrong. It bears particular attention.

Work with the Fletcher Henderson Orchestra is crucial in Armstrong's repertoire. In these recordings, James Lincoln Collier says, Armstrong showed that he "had the keenest sense of architecture of any player in the history of jazz." The solos are not just ad-libbed, they are designed and constructed. But they have the freedom, the swing, that someone who is able to improvise can apply to a song, exploring aspects of the melody, harmony, and rhythm previously undiscovered by other musicians. Collier remarked of some of Armstrong's later music, "What astonished listeners then, and continues to astonish us today, is the endless invention. For measure after measure it is all new, all different, full of unexpected leaps and turns. There are no clichés here, no falling back on the obvious to fill a momentary lack of imagination; yet it is all logical and fitting as well. Out they tumble, these bright new figures, fresh and shining as sunlight dancing on moving water." It is especially important to listen to "Sugarfoot Stomp," which made Henderson's reputation as a nationally important bandleader and which shows how Armstrong's solos drew from and surpassed his old teacher, Joe Oliver. "Sugarfoot Stomp" was based on Oliver's song "Dippermouth Blues."

To many fans and critics, the Armstrong recordings for the OKeh record company with the Hot Five and Hot Seven groups are the indispensable evidence of his greatness. Collier calls this output "one of the most significant bodies of American recorded music." He devotes an entire chapter of his book to analyzing the various sessions Armstrong led with these musicians, illuminating in painstaking detail the many nuances of the music and Armstrong's growth as a soloist and bandleader.

Any student of Armstrong's work should pay special attention to the version of "West End Blues" that emerged
from these sessions. It shows him at the height of his musical powers and also at a crossroads. He was saying goodbye
to the old style of the New Orleans bands that meant so
much to him and to many fans of jazz. He was saying in this
song and many others in these sessions that he was headed
somewhere else musically. He would take many fans with
him, but they would have to be people who liked more than
just the music people were beginning to consider traditional
jazz. Collier calls this recording "one of the masterworks of
twentieth-century music. . . . If Armstrong had not done it
before, he demonstrated now to musicians and the growing
jazz public, without the possibility of argument, that jazz
was something more than a music to drink and dance to."
He showed with "West End Blues" that jazz had endless possibilities for the expression of a wide range of emotions, delicate and heartfelt as well as raucous and jubilant.

Armstrong's December 1929 version of the "St. Louis
Blues," recorded in Chicago for OKeh, deserves special attention. He was playing with Luis Russell's band at the time.
The performance features every element of the rollicking
jazz Armstrong was developing. It begins with a section employing a Latin beat, reflecting both the general popularity
of Latin rhythms in the country at the time and the special
role of Latin American and Caribbean music in Armstrong's
hometown. Many people have referred to New Orleans as
the "northernmost Latin American city," and the opening
and subsequent sections of this version of the "St. Louis
Blues" are a tribute to that reality. It also features the great
trombonist and Armstrong pal J. C. Higginbotham amidst
the New Orleans–style polyphony so often heard in jazz of
the period.

This version also demonstrates the presence of the "boogie-woogie" bass pattern years before most people believe it appeared. The bass is played by George "Pops" Foster, one of the greats. The recording features Armstrong at his best, both on the trumpet and with the vocal solo. His trumpet playing is not ornate, but it is infectious, driving home the last sections of the song. His vocal goes in and out of the scat singing style that he essentially turned into a jazz dialect. It is almost English, not that it matters, but it turns what for many people would be a sad song into a joyous riot. This version should be compared to a couple of instrumental versions the band recorded the same day. It may also be set against Armstrong's January 1925 duet with Bessie Smith, which takes the "blues" in "St. Louis Blues" with earnest seriousness.

Armstrong's swing-era music, especially the RCA Victor recordings, are remarkable for their arrangements. Especially in the early 1930s numbers, the lush harmonies, grand introductions, and often relaxed tempos seem almost formulaic after the earlier music—which, it must be said, grew out of a certain number of formulas itself. The listener should compare Armstrong's version of the "Dusky Stevedore" with the one recorded by Emmett Miller and his Georgia Crackers. The African-American group performs a song about a black worker with gravity, compared to Miller's minstrel-style vocal. One should also compare the Armstrong band's version of "Sweet Sue" with that of Django Reinhardt and Stephane Grappelli. This pop song is swung by both groups of musicians in the "hot" style.

Practically anything Armstrong recorded with the All Stars will illuminate the watershed sensibility with which he regarded the body of his music. The All Stars do not so much bridge gaps between jazz and pop music as they make those gaps irrelevant. Again, it is especially instructive to listen to versions by the All Stars of songs Armstrong had recorded earlier, particularly "Ain't Misbehavin'" and "Back o' Town Blues."

The music of Armstrong's later years includes, of course, "Hello Dolly." His evergreen appeal is evidenced by the fact that his songs pop up in movie soundtracks, sometimes even rising to the level of hits long after his death in 1971. Two examples of this phenomenon are his recordings of "What a Wonderful World," used in the movie *Good Morning, Vietnam*, and "A Kiss to Build a Dream On," used in *Sleepless in Seattle*. Armstrong continues to be "discovered" by new fans of his music and of his unique style as a performer, as heard in all three of these songs, which are so different from one another.

The long-playing albums Armstrong made include a number of duets and other combinations, some with performers he had been at odds with from time to time, including Sammy Davis, Jr., and Duke Ellington. Some of these recordings, as Gary Giddins says, sound as if they were produced by "cornballs." Some are more sophisticated. The issue, like so many others related to Armstrong's musical choices and legacies, comes down to a matter of personal taste. Enough people liked the "cornball" material that it sold records, which meant producers wanted to record more of it, which brought still more cornball sessions. To Armstrong, it was all music. Some of it was memorable; some, even to him, was not. But he made it his own.

A Note on Sources

LOUIS ARMSTRONG'S LIFE has received a great deal of attention in print, much of it passionately expressed. Various books on his life differ about its details because of a lack of documentation at the time the books were written, the constant presence of promotional fiction, and the fact that Armstrong and his colleagues often remembered events differently and sometimes changed their accounts over time. James Lincoln Collier's *Louis Armstrong: An American Genius* (New York: Oxford University Press, 1983) is outstanding in many respects. Collier is a highly trained musician—a horn player, in fact. His sharp ear and extensive knowledge both of the sweep of jazz history and the technicalities of playing a brass instrument give him remarkable insights into the composition and execution of Armstrong's music, especially in its recorded forms. His expositions of particular recordings are quite detailed, sometimes overwhelmingly so, and highly instructive. Collier criticizes Armstrong for moving away from jazz, though not as intently or as viciously as many critics. But on the whole he is sympathetic to Armstrong, man and artist, finding him a flawed, insecure, and sometimes aloof person who was, as the title of the book says, a musical genius. Collier also places Armstrong in the broad sweep of U.S. history—a towering public figure, an icon, an *American* genius.

Gary Giddins's book *Satchmo* (New York: Doubleday, 1988), appeared five years later and benefited from newfound documents. Giddins takes on the birth date and other details of Armstrong's early life with the earnest determination of a genealogist. He tolerates Armstrong's forays into the world of popular song and away from the heady territory of jazz. His book includes many photo-

graphs, some previously unpublished, and an extensive reproduc-
tion of pages from Armstrong's autobiographical writings, which
are telling, hilarious, and touching.

Many books about Armstrong feature quotes from his writings. Some consist almost completely of things he wrote or is said
to have written. One of those is *Satchmo: My Life in New Orleans* (New York: Prentice-Hall, 1954). Among several Armstrong
memoirs and autobiographies, this one deals with his early life.
I used the Da Capo Centennial Edition from 1986, which has an
introduction by Dan Morgenstern, who argues that the book was
truly written by Armstrong himself, not a ghostwriter. However
the book came to be, it reflects Armstrong's memories and what
he wished to express about his early life. Letters that Armstrong
wrote could strike a level of formality that differed dramatically
from the slangy street speech he often used in interviews and live
performances. My favorite example of this kind of speech is part
of a radio routine from the 1940s where he and one of his musicians wonder why the word "ain't" is frowned upon. Armstrong
says, "Do you know why they don't want you to say 'ain't'?" His
straight man says, "Why?" And Armstrong says, "'Cause it ain't
right!" If the reader can occasionally suspend disbelief, *Satchmo* is
rewarding reading. Armstrong had a gift for colorful language and is
believed to have coined a number of popular jazz expressions, calling other musicians "cat" and "Pops," and originating the terms
"jive," "scat," "chops," and "gutbucket." His writing shows the
thinking and composition of someone with an unconventional,
graphic, but often graceful prose style.

Laurence Bergreen's *Louis Armstrong: An Extravagant Life*
(New York: Broadway Books, 1997) offers many details of Armstrong's early life and an excellent treatment of how New Orleans,
at the time of Armstrong's birth, had grown to be "the most international, least American of cities." Bergreen is patient with
Armstrong's musical choices. The book also has an excellent
discography.

Many writers have explored Armstrong's life and career in helpful volumes. I found beneficial Max Jones and John Chilton's *Louis:
The Louis Armstrong Story, 1900–1971* (New York: Da Capo Press,
1988); Steven Brower's *Satchmo: The Wonderful World and Art of
Louis Armstrong* (New York: Abrams, 2009); and Michael Meckna's

Satchmo: The Louis Armstrong Encyclopedia (New York: Greenwood Press, 2004). Armstrong's own *Swing That Music* (New York: Da Capo Press, 1993, reissue) is evocative but widely considered to have been heavily ghostwritten.

Several books placing jazz and Armstrong in broader contexts are available. Two I found especially helpful are Krin Gabbard's *Hotter Than That: The Trumpet, Jazz, and American Culture* (New York: Faber and Faber, 2008), which makes an especially interesting exploration of the phenomenon of masculinity in jazz trumpet playing; and William Howland Kenney, *Jazz on the River* (Chicago: University of Chicago Press, 2005), which explores the riverboat settings of early jazz. A book-length discography, unfortunately titled, is Hans Westerberg, *Boy from New Orleans: A Discography of Louis "Satchmo" Armstrong: On Records, Films, Radio, and Television* (Copenhagen: Jazzmedia, 1981). Westerberg's book covers all the recording and broadcast media that existed during Armstrong's career.

Michael Cogswell's *Louis Armstrong: The Offstage Story of Satchmo* (Portland, Ore.: Collectors Press, 2003) has a scrapbook feel because it came from materials in the Louis Armstrong Archives at Queens College in New York City. Cogswell was head of the archives. The book's extraordinary photographs give an intimate sense of Armstrong's humanity.

An article by Ben Alexander, "'For Posterity': The Personal Audio Recordings of Louis Armstrong" (*American Archivist*, Spring/Summer 2008), describes Armstrong's decades-long practice of creating and cataloging tape recordings. Alexander also pays tribute to Armstrong's memoir-writing style when he notes that "Armstrong's audio recordings relate a process of relaxed composition distinct from the more precise articulations that mark his autobiographical writings."

Hugues Panassie's book *Louis Armstrong* (New York: Charles Scribner's Sons, 1971) offers the view of a French admirer of Armstrong's in the immediate aftermath of the great artist's death. Panassie deserves to be read if only because he founded the remarkable Hot Club de France in Paris in 1932, the principal European proving ground for jazz.

Thomas Brothers's *Louis Armstrong's New Orleans* (New York: W. W. Norton, 2006) provides more insights into the city that imprinted on Armstrong so much of his music and his sense of what was right and wrong about life, work, and the desire for freedom. Brothers has a more nuanced view of ragtime than most writers. He has also written *Louis Armstrong, in His Own Words* (New York: Oxford University Press, 1999), which consists of mostly verbatim reprints of Armstrong's letters, memoir fragments, and other autobiographical comments that flowed from his beloved typewriter.

Armstrong's sense of his own history shines through in these and other writings, suggesting why it was important to him to tell as much of his story as possible. In many ways he controlled his own destiny, especially in his determination to choose the kind of music he wanted. But in other ways he recognized that he controlled little about his life, and through his personal writings he sought to influence how his story would be told.

Index

Illustrations are indicated with *italics*.

A NOTE ON THE AUTHOR

David Stricklin directs the Butler Center for Arkansas Studies in Little Rock and is adjunct professor of history at the University of Arkansas
there. Born in Cleburne, Texas, he studied at Bay-
lor University and Tulane University, where he
received a Ph.D. in American history. He has also
written *A Genealogy of Dissent*, about Southern
Baptist protest in the twentieth century, and, with
Bill C. Malone, *Southern Music/American Music*.
He is married with two daughters and lives in
Little Rock.